ALCHEMICAL LIGHTWORK

"There are books that capture the longings and hopes of a pivotal era in history and give them a form that catalyzes collective change. *Alchemical Lightwork* may well fill that role for our time. Combining the contemporary spiritual movement of lightwork with the wisdom of classical alchemical texts, this book offers a path out of the darkness of our 'enlightened' dark age toward individual and collective spiritual regeneration."

John Michael Greer, author of *The King in Orange*,
The Twilight of Pluto, *The Druidry Handbook*,
and *The Way of the Golden Section*

"This luminous book weaves light, love, and creativity into a network of associations that enhance and support human spiritual development. Versluis traces the various stages of alchemical transformation for the integration of the inner and outer, of the soul and body, through 'steps of light' leading to wholeness and unity. This book synthesizes alchemical history, leading figures, deep symbolism, visual art, and sacred texts with a hidden history of elemental, esoteric teachings and ancient mysteries. A passionate counternarrative to the current spiritual uncertainty, this book offers a brilliant reformulation of alchemy as a path of personal spiritual discovery. Beautifully illustrated with rare alchemical prints, this is an inspiring guide to inner transformation!"

Lee Irwin, author of *Alchemy of Soul*
and *Divine Feminine Gnosis*

"Through the ancient craft of spiritual alchemy, Arthur Versluis guides us on a journey through stages of restoration both physical and mystical. This is an important book that can initiate profound changes both within us and in the world. Highly recommended."

JOHN MATTHEWS, AUTHOR OF *THE PROPHECIES OF MERLIN* AND COAUTHOR OF *THE COMPLETE KING ARTHUR* AND *THE LOST BOOK OF THE GRAIL*

"This is a truly light-filled book that speaks to our nigredo age in the language of alchemical transmutation, lighting the way to a restored wholeness for ourselves and our society."

CHRISTOPHER MCINTOSH, AUTHOR OF *THE CALL OF THE OLD GODS*, *OCCULT RUSSIA*, AND *OCCULT GERMANY*

"I recommend this book—with its superb color illustrations—to any reader or student of alchemy who seeks to move beyond the endless repetitions found in contemporary publications."

R. J. STEWART, AUTHOR OF *EARTH LIGHT*, *THE UNDERWORLD INITIATION*, AND *ADVANCED MAGICAL ARTS*

ALCHEMICAL LIGHTWORK

A GUIDE TO CREATING CULTURES OF LIGHT
~ AND ~
SPIRITUAL AWAKENING

Arthur Versluis

Destiny Books
Rochester, Vermont

Destiny Books
One Park Street
Rochester, Vermont 05767
www.DestinyBooks.com

Destiny Books is a division of Inner Traditions International

Copyright © 2025 by Arthur Versluis

All rights reserved. No part of this book may be reproduced or utilized in any form or by any means, electronic or mechanical, including photocopying, recording, or any information storage and retrieval system, without permission in writing from the publisher. No part of this book may be used or reproduced to train artificial intelligence technologies or systems.

Cataloging-in-Publication Data for this title is available from the Library of Congress

ISBN 979-8-88850-018-7 (print)
ISBN 979-8-88850-019-4 (ebook)

Printed and bound in the United States by Lake Book Manufacturing, LLC

10 9 8 7 6 5 4 3 2 1

Text design by Debbie Glogover and layout by Kira Kariakin
This book was typeset with Garamond Premier Pro with Adobe Carslon Pro, Anchsara, Celestia Antiqua Std, Dutch Mediaeval Pro, Gill Sans MT Pro, ITC Legacy Sans Std used as display typefaces.

To send correspondence to the author of this book, mail a first-class letter to the author c/o Inner Traditions, One Park Street, Rochester, VT 05767, and we will forward the communication. View the author's website by visiting arthurversluis.com.

Scan the QR code and save 25% at InnerTraditions.com. Browse over 2,000 titles on spirituality, the occult, ancient mysteries, new science, holistic health, and natural medicine.

There are spiritual, intellectual, and sensible perfections of light. The first is that inaccessible light which sees all things, but is comprehended by nothing. The second is a spiritual reality, whose nature possesses no place, yet is entirely whole in every part of his circumscription. By the third we understand the sensible perfection of the sun, moon, and stars. Because heaven and earth differ not essentially, being originally from one chaos, but in the order of beings and prime termination. Therefore kings, rulers and magistrates, and others eminent in charge, are called lights, as having relation to supreme light.
    Patrick Scot, *The Tillage of Light*

Matter . . . is the house of light. . . . When [light] first enters it, it is a glorious, transparent room, a crystal castle, and he lives like a familiar in diamonds. . . . At last the earth grows over him out of the water, so he is quite shut up in darkness.

Thomas Vaughan, *Aula Lucis*

He that desires to be happy let him look after light, for it is the cause of happiness, both temporal and eternal. . . . Nature herself dictates to us that our happiness consists in light.

Thomas Vaughan, *Aula Lucis*

Contents

Tabula Smaragdina: *Emerald Tablet of Hermes Trismegistus*   x

Introduction: The *Emerald Tablet* and the Path of Light   1

PART ONE
The Black

1. The End of an Age   12
2. Alchemy: The Steps of Light   20
3. The Astral Shell   30
4. The Burdens We Carry   39

PART TWO
The White

5. The Light of Nature   48
6. Turning toward Earth   57
7. The Transmutative Process   65

PART THREE
THE YELLOW

| 8 | The Mysteries Reborn | 76 |
| 9 | Light Eternal | 84 |

PART FOUR
THE RED

10	Seeding New Cultures	94
11	Restoring Wholeness and Flourishing	103
12	A Vision	111

Appendix 1: Additional Resources	127
Appendix 2: An Alchemical Community	129
Appendix 3: *Dialogues* and Illumination	137

Further Readings	145
Index	146
About the Author	149

TABULA SMARAGDINA

Emerald Tablet of Hermes Trismegistus

1. I speak not fictitious things, but what is true and most certain.
2. What is below is like that which is above, and what is above is like that which is below, accomplishing the miracles of One.
3. All things come from the mediation of One, so are all things born from this One.
4. Its father is the Sun, its mother is the Moon. The wind carries it in its belly; the earth nourishes it.
5. It causes works of wonder (*telesmi*) and is the completion of the whole world.
6. Its power is complete if it be turned toward earth.
7. Separating the earth from the fire, the subtle from the gross, with care and ingenuity.
8. Ascend wisely from the earth to heaven, and then again descend to earth, uniting what is above and below. Thus you will realize the glory of the whole world, and all obscurity and darkness will fly far away from you.
9. This is the power of all powers, as it overcomes all that is subtle, and permeates everything solid.
10. Thus is everything created.
11. From here proceed wonderful adaptations, of which this is the process.
12. Therefore I am called Hermes Trismegistus, having the three parts of the philosophy of the whole world.
13. That which I had to say concerning the operation of the Sun is completed.

INTRODUCTION

The *Emerald Tablet* and the Path of Light

> *I speak not fictitious things, but what is true and most certain.*
>
> EMERALD TABLET

In a dream, many years ago, I was given a numinous book—one bound in ancient leather and wood covers bearing many enigmatic luminous alchemical glyphs, and held together with a special clasp—to convey into the future. To this day, I can still see it clearly in my mind's eye. In the dream, I accepted that responsibility—or to put it more exactly, the dream described what I was actually doing. Already by that time, I had spent many years engaged in working with little-known traditions in inner alchemy, meaning ways of visualizing and working with spiritual images in a process of inner transformation and awakening. So when I shared the dream with a close friend working in the tradition of inner alchemy, he replied that it made perfect sense. The dream reflected something very real, and he understood that intuitively. This book is one manifestation of that dream.

What is this book about? Ultimately, it is about our individual and shared future. Someone reading this book likely has come to recognize cracks in what was once our familiar world. Outwardly, there appear to be many reasons for pessimism. Materialistic progress exists, of course, but anyone can see that inherent in our outward technological power, for all its apparent magic, is also the destruction of nature, of cultures, indeed, of what it means to be human and to flourish with nature. Outwardly, our world is ailing, and inwardly, we know something is deeply wrong.

What is wrong will not be fixed by technology. Artificial pseudo-worlds might divert some people for a time and might be lucrative for those who produce and control them, but artificial intelligence along with artificial "reality" is just that: artifice. It is illusion and delusion atop an exploitive technological system, and neither we nor nature can flourish in such a system—the very idea is laughable. A very different direction is necessary.

Many of what are proposed as "green" solutions to the ecological destruction being wrought around the world actually are extensions of the very system that produced the destruction. For instance, the process of extracting the minerals needed to produce electric cars creates vast pit mines and is essentially just another industrial exploitation system that actually does more harm to the environment than the benefit of electric cars can balance out. There is no quarter given to culture or spirituality in such a system. The fundamental problem is that an authentic path forward can't come from within the closed loop of the system itself.

There have been experiments involving more ecologically sound and sustainable communities from the hippie era onward, and of course many before that, though the vast majority of them, being communal, collapsed relatively swiftly. In this century, new models for ecovillages have been developed. These new models are not communistic but rather encourage individual and family groupings in an area or region so that aspirations and orientations can be shared without losing individual ownership and familial continuity.

These ecovillage experiments and related secession movements of various kinds are a major step forward. However, while we see such ecovillage or intentional community experiments emerging, they are often without any distinctive cultural and spiritual orientation. Sustainability is all very well, but divorced from spirituality and culture, it is truncated—really an extension of the system that produced it—and cannot flourish. Something more is necessary; we know that instinctively. Flourishing means that we grow and prosper as creative human beings on a spiritual path toward awakening, in a thriving natural world.

A wild array of contemporary ideas and theories circulate in social media and in new age books or websites, variants waxing and waning in popularity, often announcing an imminent new age, some derived from quantum physics, multidimensionality, 5-D, starseeds, galactic communiqués, or other variants of "channeling." These and many other ideas and perspectives emerge, become popular, and then wane as their replacements wax in turn. They are presented as exciting and new. At the same time, they are also presented in ways that appear disconnected from our shared human cultural and spiritual riches.

One aspect of this book is to suggest how one recent development, "lightworking," or working with and in light, can be understood in relation to the profound and ancient tradition of alchemy, especially Western alchemy, which can be traced back into the distant past. Contemporary lightworking is generally intuitively understood as heeding an inner calling to radiate light and love, and avoid getting caught up in dark, materialistic, and fear-driven selfishness. Through the ancient wisdom tradition of alchemy we can understand this calling more deeply. Alchemy, which centers on color, light, and illumination, offers us an understanding of light and how to work with it in our own spiritual practice and our own movement toward awakening.

Even if we already have learned about or have experience in working with light, alchemy provides us with invaluable images, symbols, parables, texts, and guidance for spiritual practice in relation to nature, other people, and ultimately a transmuted individual, community, and world. Alchemy provides us with a larger map and with a sense of direction. Drawing on the ancient alchemical tradition, we begin to see how we can move toward illumination and develop a vibrant spiritual community in a flourishing natural world.

What is the essential message of alchemy? It is that we human beings are fallen, but can be restored, and that likewise the world is in decline, or fallen, but it also can be restored. What is the means of renewing individuals, cultures, and nature? The alchemical process of illumination, conveyed through symbols and riddles. Alchemy returns us, returns the world, to original purity.

Alchemy is understood to unfold in colored stages, from the black, to the white, to the yellow, to the red. It is the unveiling of the light. But the process is not linear, going like a train from here to there. Rather, it unfolds in a spiral, where we return to the same place but in a new way, as the spiral unfolds. Alchemy ultimately is the unveiling of that which always was there, and it is conveyed in enigmatic, pure images of primordial nature and human beings. Hence its fascinating power. We can return to it, and to this book, and see things anew each time for the first time. It belongs to and calls us to a different way of being in the world.

Alchemy can be traced back several thousand years, and we will here be drawing on some of the earliest alchemical works that have come down to us. Alchemy can be understood in different ways. Yes, it includes ways of working with minerals and plants through heating and distillation in order to restore us and the world around us to an original paradisal harmony. And it also includes, in enigmatic images and texts, the stages of spiritual awakening.

But one can't go successfully to alchemical texts and images as if they were a series of laboratory directions alone, a kind of proto-chemistry. Alchemy requires a different approach that isn't materialistic or only rationalistic. Rather, alchemical images and texts are symbolic and dreamlike—they call us to a transmuted way of being in the world. This book is also like that: you will discover new insights with each foray into it.

An essential concept for understanding alchemy more deeply is *initiation*. But what does *initiation* mean? The word itself conveys the idea of a new beginning, initiating a new cycle or process. Alchemy *initiates* a transformative process. The word also can convey the initiatory process itself, in this sense meaning a challenging process of transmutation from a fallen to an unfallen, or restored, nature. In this second sense, the word *initiation* conveys a sometimes difficult process of breakdown and regeneration.

And there is still a third sense of *initiation*: entry into a lineage in a tradition. This tradition of alchemy, which began in timelessness, was revealed to an alchemical practitioner, who passed it along to another, who passed it along to another. The Western alchemical tradition is understood to be under the sign of Hermes Trismegistus (Thrice-Great Hermes) who is the perpetual initiator into alchemy's secrets, and who, as we see in the *Emerald Tablet*, is the revealer of its mysteries. Initiation is also collaboration. I know several experienced practitioners of alchemy, one of whom I have collaborated with for many years, and we work within a branch of a much larger and longer Hermetic tradition.

It is important to understand that what we as individuals do does not occur only in the context of our own lives. There is a greater context that we must recognize and understand. Ultimately, we must think and act not only for ourselves but for our shared prosperity in the future. There is a better way to live—not only for us individually, but for all of us—and this book offers suggestions for new shared, primordial ways of being and flourishing in the world.

It is all about vision. Not *a* vision or *the* vision, but vision itself—that is, the ability to *see*. There are different kinds of vision, of course. There is what we clearly see with our eyes when we look out at fields and woods on a sunny day. Then there is recognizing what is within and beyond what we see with our eyes; seeing with the eyes of the spirit into hidden aspects of nature. And then, beyond these, there is vision as guidance, in the sense of envisioning, seeing what is possible, envisioning the future. We need each of these kinds of vision, and alchemical lightwork awakens all three.

Of course, this book can only be an introduction to alchemical lightwork. It gives experiential indications of how to practice, but everyone must engage in the individual work themselves. Alchemy is a path of transmutation and has many aspects and dimensions, and we will be drawing on some specific images and works to understand the process, but it is up to the reader to then explore and engage in it.

I am only the conveyor of what is in this book. The alchemical tradition already exists, the light always is, but I have been fortunate to encounter it and am in a position to share some of its aspects. All of this goes beyond any individual, and in time you may begin to see even your own individual transmutation as, paradoxically, not really your own but as part of a much greater process that transcends our apparent identities in this world.

In the Himalayas, there is a tradition of forging ritual implements in part out of meteoric iron. These implements are held to have a special kind of otherworldly power. The alchemical tradition drawn upon in this book is more than a little like those ritual tools made in part from meteors. It appears, trailing clouds of glory from another world into this one, out of the blue. It is both otherworldly and worldly.

How do we begin to heal and transform ourselves, those around us, and our relationship to the natural and spiritual realms? We have been given ways to accomplish this healing and transmutation process, and these can be found in alchemical works that are largely hidden from public knowledge and are vital contributions to the Western European spiritual tradition.

The Hermetic alchemical tradition is distinct from religious traditions such as Christianity or Islam but can be expressed in a Christian or Islamic religious context, as in the case of Christian theosophic alchemy in the tradition of the great Christian mystic Jacob Böhme (1575–1624). We often see Christian themes or symbols in the European alchemical tradition during its great efflorescence in the sixteenth, seventeenth, and eighteenth centuries, and in the tradition of Jacob Böhme we see the entire alchemical process condensed into and understood as the heart of the Christian process of spiritual regeneration and illumination. This book draws from essential alchemical source works, and especially from the *Emerald Tablet*, but these sources are applied here in a novel way, for a different time and circumstance.

There are different kinds of alchemical sources. Some are texts and images in the European tradition, some harking back to antiquity, while others belong to the amazing period of alchemical flourishing in the seventeenth and eighteenth centuries. Another source is guidance from someone who has a deeper understanding of those images and texts, their inner meanings, and what they mean in practice. This book reflects all of these, since it weaves together alchemical texts and images with the guidance I have been given from a longtime practitioner.

The *Emerald Tablet* provides the leitmotif for all that follows in this book, which also includes the alchemical tradition of spiritual awakening as outlined and depicted in the great works of alchemical imagery such as the *Aurora Consurgens* (where we see the *Emerald Tablet* depicted), *Splendor Solis*, and the *Rosarium Philosophorum* (*The Rose Garden of the Philosophers*). This book, *Alchemical Lightwork*, includes never-before-published illustrations from the *Rosarium* showing the stages of spiritual awakening as the transformation and union of a divine couple and draws from very rare spiritual alchemical texts, all understood as expressions of the path of light expressed in the seminal *Emerald Tablet*.

Together, you and I will approach the path of the *Emerald Tablet* as fellow explorers who individually and together engage with this rich, extraordinary world. To do this, we need to drop our preconceptions and judgment and see with new eyes. Not everyone is ready for this journey, but if you are, then let's set forth as coexplorers. I say "coexplorer" because this is a different kind of approach than you may be familiar with, and it calls for a new name. I am not presenting myself as a sage. Rather, I am offering you the opportunity to join me on a journey that goes beyond us as isolated individuals, engaging us each in sharing our exploration of a vast new luminous and spiritual terrain. If you are called to this journey, then it is as a coexplorer.

There were certainly many people in the past who were familiar with what is in this book. We are not the first to explore its depths, and we are not, by virtue of living now, better or wiser than they were. Sophisticated devices don't bring inner experience or wisdom. In fact, they distract us. Someone living in an earlier age may well have been able to naturally awaken spiritually by virtue of their closeness to nature and nature's rhythms, for their lives also were suffused with ancient folk tradition and cultural richness.

What we have lost, we can recover, and indeed, must recover or, to put it more accurately, renew. If you are reading this, and it resonates with you, then you recognize the calling. But a calling to what? It stirs in us, and yet we don't quite know which direction to go in. It's difficult, in our confused and lost society, to find our way to something real. But we know in our heart that it must be possible. And we know intuitively that it is about light.

Is it only happenstance that in the West sages are *illuminated* and in the East they are *enlightened*? Alchemical images and treatises also refer to the light, to illumination, and to a process marked by different colors of light. Could this really refer merely to the light we see on a sunny day? What did the alchemist Thomas Vaughan mean when he wrote that "matter . . . is the house of light," and that light is the cause of both temporal and eternal happiness? Of course, we enjoy seeing the sunlight on a beautiful day, and moonlight at night. But is this the happiness to which he is referring?

You can see we're presented immediately with enigmas. Alchemical works consist of enigmas wrapped in allusions. Why is this? Perhaps because our consciousness responds best to tantalizing symbols and images and to dreamlike communications, and some part of us long asleep begins to stir and awaken when we work with them. A dualistic approach, using the logic that can make an earthmover or a mining pit, can't grasp it, let alone explicate it. Rather, we're talking about something that is best conveyed in literature and song, in beautifully illustrated works of art, in folktales and mystery. But this is what disappears in an ever more lost society.

The *Emerald Tablet* begins with a single declaration: "I speak not fictitious things, but what is true and most certain." In other words, what it speaks of is not projected or confected but genuinely true. It reflects how things really are, behind the scenes. Western alchemy represents a fundamentally different understanding of the nature of our world and of ourselves than that asserted in a materialistic era. Of course, materialists will say that it is fictional, but the *Emerald Tablet* begins by rejecting that claim.

The idea that "matter is the house of light" offers an ancient and profound, unified way of understanding nature. In this perspective, matter and spirit are not divided. Rather, nature originates from light and is pervaded by it. Matter is illuminated from within. Intuitively, we recognize what this means. It is a poetic way of expressing a Hermetic understanding of nature, but to fully understand it experientially, we have to go on a quest.

In the Grail tradition, you might recall, the knight Parzival arrives at the magical castle Munsalvaesche, where he is invited to a dinner in the great hall. At the dinner, the knights are disconsolate, and it is obvious something is awry in the kingdom. Then King Anfortas is brought in, wounded and ill, lying on a cot. The queen brings in the holy grailstone, which is translucent garnet hyacinth, and it manifests magical food and drink for all. But Parzival does not ask the Question that would have brought about the healing. The next morning, after a troubled night, he discovers that nearly all have left the castle, and his cousin Sigune, who remains, chides him for having failed to ask Anfortas the Question, and Parzival feels great remorse.

What is the Question? The Question is: What ails us all? What has gone awry in the kingdom? What is wrong? Like Parzival, we can see that something is amiss in our world. Instinctively, we know it. But we don't articulate it. We continue in our familiar rut, we keep our head down, and even if we notice what is wrong, we don't say it out loud or bring it into wider consciousness, especially if it's systemic. To ask the Question takes courage as well as wisdom. But asking the Question is only the first step. It is not enough just to recognize what has gone wrong. We need clear seeing. We need vision to guide us. What does a healed kingdom look like? What do we envision? We have to be able to see from here to *there*. Alchemical transmutation is not only about us as apparently discrete individuals. As we will see, and as is clear in the Grail tradition, it is the healing and restoration of the whole kingdom, that is, of the realms of nature and culture in the light of the spirit. In order for that to happen, we need to see it, and see our way to it.

If we are to create healthy cultures in the future, they will be built on the spiritual cornerstone rejected by the builders of the society we see now. Ultimately, this book is about how to accomplish this. It comes about not through top-down systemic fiat but through inspiration and small groups, through manifesting vision individually, in couples, and in communities. It encourages vision for what comes *after* the hard times. It encourages vision for the golden age on the other side of the dark age.

But we begin with where we are now.

PART ONE
THE BLACK

1
The End of an Age

What is below is like that which is above, and what is above is like that which is below, accomplishing the miracles of one.

EMERALD TABLET

Something has changed. We can feel it. We know it in our bones. Before, we could still believe in the machine system or, at least to some degree, we could rationalize some provisional belief in it. Now, we can see around us the fissures in the edifice. It has been a long time coming. More than a century ago, poets recognized that the advent of "modernity" meant the dissolution of ancient ways of being. But now we have entered a new phase.

What is this new phase? Is it the coming of a long night, a dark age, or the dawn of a new era? We have been told that the period after the fall of Rome was a dark age. But was it? It all depends on how we see, and what measure we apply. Of course, if we measure by technological magic, then the more sophisticated the machines, the more advanced we are. We might have an almost religious faith in "progress" or "evolution," and if so, we might convince ourselves that given the rapid advance of technology these days, we cannot possibly be entering a dark age.

But we can also measure by happiness, as proposed by Jigme Singye Wangchuck, the fourth king of Bhutan. Famously, he called for life to be measured not by GNP but by GNH—Gross National Happiness. Of course, such a measure naturally evokes the question: Are you and the people around you happier today than you were in the past? What is your locale's or country's GNH level today compared to ten years ago? Or to a hundred?

More technology does not seem to correlate to more happiness, does it? It seems the more technology people have in their lives, the less happy they are. In fact, as the system entered into Bhutan, that beautiful hidden land's people began to suffer in new ways, as with it came drugs, crime, and cracks in the foundation of Bhutan's culture.

Does technology, including virtual forms like social media, contribute to our individual and collective happiness? Or is it actually a source of unhappiness? I presented a series of public events introducing meditation practice to undergraduate university students, and as part of this I mentioned the many surveys showing that their generation was the most psychologically wounded on record, the most distressed. One national poll found that nearly a third of young women of high school age had contemplated suicide within the previous year. I asked the students whether this was true, and if so, why. Their answers were interesting.

I asked, "Why are so many of us fragile and distressed?"

"Because we are addicted to social media," one said. "We are always looking at our devices."

"It's not only that," said another. "It's because we see our friends are putting on a false face about their successes and happiness, and when we see that, we become depressed because it's not like that for us. Social media is designed to give us a thrill, to keep us addicted, but it also makes us miserable."

"That's true," someone else said. "But I can't quit my devices."

"Me neither," said another.

I was surprised by their unanimity and inspired by their strong interest in making a change individually.

But what about society in broader terms?

CAUGHT IN THE TIDE

There are two diametrically opposed movements in contemporary society. One is toward more and more centralized power and control, and the other is toward decentralization and renewal of archaic ways of being. One is toward ever greater illusion, the other toward reality. One is deception, the other, truth. One disconnects us from the natural world, the other restores our deep understanding of it.

We are caught like swimmers in the currents of a great tidal wave. Those tidal currents are much stronger than we are as individuals, and the conflict is intensified by technology, which makes the currents virtually irresistible. They carry us along in their inexorable grip, attempting to pull us out to the sea of perdition. I have observed very few who have the strength to resist, let alone to fight to shore and up out of the waters to freedom and safety. Very few. But alchemy can provide us with some guidance in this struggle.

The alchemical process offers us a way of understanding the larger cycle of human creativity beginning where we are today in society as a whole—in the stage of dissolution, decomposition. This is the first stage in the alchemical process and is called *nigredo*, the darkness, the black. Part of this stage is becoming aware not only of *what* has gone wrong in our life, but *how*. What, in how we see the world, has led us astray?

When we are caught in society's conflicting currents, we are in a continuously reactive mode, and we don't see things as they are. We react with anger, fear, or desire; we attach, avoid, or reject. We identify as a subject reacting to whatever or whoever is in our purview, and this reaction might be angry, or fearful, or desirous.

Jacob Böhme addressed this in his discussion of the alchemical process in *The Signature of All Things*. In the first phase, the nigredo, the dark astrological triad of Saturn, Mars, and Mercury, is dominant. Saturn symbolizes the contractive, controlling energy of the psyche; Mars symbolizes the psyche's angry energy; and Mercury symbolizes the judgmental, mercurial nature of the ego, constantly asking whether this is good for me or bad. This is the dominance of the superficial personality, which is shaped by the world and which reacts to the world. It is all about self. How do *I* look in the mirror of the world? How can *I* look better?

In Christian terms, this is our fallen state, and we need to bear in mind that there is a collective or shared aspect to "fallenness," especially if or when a people is turned against their own fundamental nature and history. We saw this when communists seized power in Russia, China, and Cambodia, for instance. Their fierce materialism in itself was not enough: the communist revolutionaries felt compelled to obliterate the past, to obliterate the spiritual, to obliterate meaning itself if they could, so as to have room for themselves to take even more power. Wearing the mantle of a feigned moral cause, they destroyed and murdered.

THE DARK

There are mysteries of iniquity. What is it that drives people to imprison, torture, and murder spiritual practitioners, to burn sacred texts and melt down sacred images, to seek to obliterate beautiful statues commemorating the past, to ban and censure? All of this is part of the nigredo phase of the alchemical process, the phase of destruction or decomposition. The breaking down. The tearing apart. It is painful. It is more painful the more aware you are of what is true, what is good, and what is beautiful.

And so we begin to think we may be in a dark age already. A true dark age is one in which truth is not only suppressed and lost to most, but criminalized. A true dark age is an age of lies. The first and paramount lie is that only materiality is real. That is the premise on which all the systems of exploitation are based—especially the ideological totalitarian ones that call themselves communism. The measure of a system's evil is the degree to which its rulers target and destroy spirituality and the culture that expresses and supports it.

This is the nigredo phase through which we must pass: it is the dark time of dissolution. What seemed solid is broken around us, and the familiar ways of centuries and millennia are obliterated. In this phase, we feel and are lost. We know something is wrong, but not how to fix it, or even if it can be fixed. We don't know what we don't know, but we know something is awry. We might seek to be a part of the system, or seek its rewards, but that doesn't bring satisfaction, let alone meaning. Where is meaning?

There are two aspects to the nigredo: one individual, and the other collective. Individually, it is of course expressed psychologically—we feel alone, depressed, lost, anxious, angry, and envious of those who seem as if they are happier than we are. We know that we need something, but aren't sure what. The collective dimension is the herd mentality. Those already in the herd want others to be part of it, insisting on it, and they are all easily driven by shouts and prods from herders, who are even more deluded than those in the herd. At heart, we realize eventually, what we need is spirituality.

But a dark age is fiercely materialistic. It reinforces the sense of self separate from other. *I* need to get *this* in order to be happy. The sense of *I* and *them* dominates how we see others, and the sense that *I* gain by exploiting "natural resources" dominates how we see the world. In both cases, materiality is the only reality. Anyone who thinks otherwise is a fool. *I* must get *mine*. This expresses the dark triad's Saturnine restriction.

Then there is Mars. Anger. Wrath. If I cannot *get*, then I am angry, and I blame. I reject. This is an even more intense dualism; the dualism of self *against* other. Wrath is not only this kind of anger, though—it also has a cosmic dimension. Wrath is the aspect of division and brokenness in our cosmos itself, cracked and shattered. There is a spiritual metahistory to this world in which we find ourselves, and it produced fallen nature and fallen humanity, caught in the now-swift currents of this dark age.

The dualism of war extends wrath into the collective, and here it is *us* and *them*. *We* must win against *them*. It is not a personalized anger; eventually, the collective expression of wrath sweeps people along with it, even though the flames are set and fanned by those in power, or putatively in power. War can be understood as a conflagration. But it is also a racket, with profits for a few, and misery for the many.

Mercury is not always part of the dark triad, as Mercury can be either light or dark, but an age of technology is mercurial and largely contributes to an era of judgment, fear, and anger amplified by broadcasting one's feelings. Scapegoating, targeting others for retribution, surveillance, and the panopticon all reflect the dark triad of these three mythic glyphs. Technology alienates us from our world and from one another even as it connects us.

FROM MATERIALISM TO NIHILISM

Materialism is delusional. It is the belief that only the physical world exists, and that when we die, there's just nothing. This leads directly into unethical beliefs about "getting what's mine" in hedonic pursuits, chasing after the accumulation of wealth or power, getting lost in distractions like games or virtual reality, harming others, harming oneself through addictive drugs, and engaging in nihilism, a belief that "nothing is true," and "everything is permitted." Such a person in a position of power could destroy a society or perhaps the entire Earth.

Materialism and nihilism go together in the prevailing secular ideology, if we can call it that. Nihilism is a mistaken belief that existence is meaningless and therefore there is no need for fundamental ethical responsibility, and there are no consequences. It is delusional, but at the same time, for a certain kind of individual, fatally attractive. Nihilism is the end result of dogmatic materialism, the mistaken belief that physical appearance is the only reality. What we call modernity is really a concerted, sustained effort to inculcate a materialist worldview, and the consequence—nihilism—followed after. All of this is a pack of lies, no matter how emphatically someone blares it.

Materialism and nihilism combine to produce still another pack of lies, which we can call a realm of illusion. This realm of artifice is created through technological means and, of course, is therefore derivative of and dependent on a materialistic technological system. It is below or inferior to the actual world, which it seeks to replace, while those who rule it are demiurges creating an inferior illusory world to replace the real one. Such realms are, in addition to being time wasters, traps for the unwary.

Some refer to a technological "metaverse," but this is not really *meta* at all, since *meta* really refers to transcendence, to a spiritual dimension eerily absent from the virtual realms created by human-generated and software-generated demiurges. The metaverse, or virtual reality, actually is *infra*, meaning below the natural and human orders, and should by rights be called an "infraverse." An infraverse is dominated ultimately by the dark triad, as it is created to exploit or pander to people's lower impulses and in its very makeup separates us from humanity and nature as well as, of course, from the spiritual.

This book points in exactly the opposite direction, away from entrapment and toward freedom, away from illusion and toward natural and spiritual reality and liberation. The alchemical tradition guides us toward becoming better human beings, toward flourishing through living in harmony with natural and spiritual realities. It is about understanding the hidden principles animating nature and ourselves and activating them so that we and others can flourish together and move toward spiritual awakening and freedom, or illumination.

THE GOLDEN AGE

We are at the end of an age, but in this end are the seeds of another to come. This book is about planting and nurturing the seeds of a coming golden age. In ancient European cosmology, time was understood to be cyclical, and it was believed that the current Iron Age (the Kali Yuga of Hinduism) is to be followed, inexorably, by a new time cycle and a new golden age. Even though things look increasingly dark, there is light and there are seeds we can tend now for the future. It is not only that a golden age is possible—it is that a golden age is inevitable. But we must tune ourselves to it and allow it to begin to manifest where we are.

What is a golden age? It is what we all seek: truth. Realizing who we authentically, primordially are and how to flourish. In an age of darkness, this may seem farfetched, but it is not. It requires, above all, changing our understanding of ourselves and others and the natural world. Golden age culture is the harmonious expression of human spirituality in nature.

Even in a time of darkness, a golden age culture is possible. How? Through religion. Religion, as understood here, orients people toward being ethical, toward becoming good. We intuitively understand what this means. Someone who is good is honest, helpful, kind, caring, and seeks to benefit others and to help his or her community flourish. But religion as understood here also has a transcendent dimension—it is not only about this life. It is about what follows this life. Ancient European religious traditions—like Buddhism and Hinduism—hold that death is not the end of life, only the end of this tenuous physical life. This understanding is the antidote to nihilism and its destructive effects.

In an age when everything appears to be falling apart, and it seems the center cannot hold, we are also given the precious opportunity to begin to forge another way of being in the world, one that directly is grounded in primordial reality and that allows us to flourish in concert with nature. That is possible now, just as it always has been. But how do we get there? Through the alchemical process indicated in the *Emerald Tablet*, which can be understood both individually and culturally as expressed in community.

In a materialistic era, people are inundated with the view that what we see is all that there is. There is no above, they say, or they refer to that which is above as somehow elitist or bad. So the first step, the *Emerald Tablet* tells us, is to recognize the reciprocity between and the ultimate unity of above and below, light and matter. We have to break through to a more profound view. This is the first step in the process of awakening.

At the same time, and at all times, as the *Emerald Tablet* puts it, what is above is always present and manifested here below, in the natural world. Humanity is not separate from nature or from spirit—these three spheres are one as they always have been. What is below is like what is above, and their union always manifests the miracles of the One. What are these miracles that the *Emerald Tablet* refers to? Are miracles possible even in a dark age? That, of course, we will explore together in what follows.

2

Alchemy: The Steps of Light

All things come from the mediation of One, so are all things born from this One.

EMERALD TABLET

For a long time now, alchemy and alchemical practices have been relegated to the drawer of discarded items. Perhaps everyone has such a drawer, filled with bric-a-brac, old devices, and small tools that one uses once in a blue moon. Some people claim that alchemy is outmoded, just protochemistry from those days in seventeenth- or eighteenth-century Europe, say, when, materialists think, benighted souls only looked greedily for some way to make themselves wealthy by transmuting lead into gold, or worked in a laboratory for who-knows-what purpose. Still, all those magnificent alchemical images, those treatises, remain stored away in our collective drawer of discarded items—not used, but not thrown away either. Here, we are going to take alchemy out of that drawer, wipe off the dust, and have a look.

Alchemy has a very long history in both the West and the East. It provides us with keys for understanding the secrets of nature and spirit, and those keys have remained remarkably similar over many centuries.

Yet alchemy is just as mysterious, enigmatic, dreamlike, elusive, and allusive now as it was millennia ago. Alchemy, both in its Western and Eastern forms, certainly includes laboratory work with herbs and metals as we know from the many detailed texts and instructions found in the Indian tradition, for example. Such laboratory work may include pulverizing, slow heating, condensing, or other means of working with natural substances to bring out, transmute, or perfect their hidden aspects. But is alchemy only laboratory work?

An ancient Greek adept named Zosimos* provides us with glimpses of alchemical work in late antiquity that bear striking similarities to those described in the classic alchemical work *Emerald Tablet* woven throughout this book. In fact, Zosimos's *Visions* begins by observing that the growth and cessation and renovation of the bodily nature, the separation and union of spirit and body, and operations with metals and plants are all of the One Nature, acting upon itself. The One Nature transforms itself. This statement is very similar to the view of the One that we find in the *Emerald Tablet*.

Zosimos goes on to provide us with a visionary account. He tells us that he slept, and in sleep saw a bowl-like altar with fifteen steps, with a sacrificial priest standing over it. From above, a voice told him that "I have completed the descent of the fifteen steps and I have ascended the steps of light. And it is the sacrificing priest that renews me, casting off the coarseness of the body, so that by necessity I have become spirit." In the altar, he later learns, all is mixed, separated, moistened and dried, budded and blossomed, and otherwise transfigured through a "natural method," "breathing in, breathing out," through a "natural

---

*Zosimos of Panopolis, who lived around 300 CE, wrote the oldest known alchemical works in the Western world. He lived in the Roman region of Egypt, and his work shows aspects of ancient Egyptian, Hermetic, and Gnostic currents. He describes alchemical work in terms of images, which we see later in European alchemical works such as *Rosarium Philosophorum*. The mysteries of alchemical transmutation are conveyed symbolically, through images, as in his *Book of Pictures*, as we also see in Zosimos's related dreams or visions. He had a female counterpart and interlocutor, Theosebeia, who is reflected in his extant letters to her.

harmony" coming to fruition through Nature's transformation of herself. Admittedly, Zosimos's vision as a whole is very strange, involving transformations and "mortifications" of "little men," and the appearance and disappearance of guides of various kinds—too much for us to go into in detail here without going astray.

But there are some points we can draw from his dreamlike story. First, we will have noticed the "steps of light" mentioned in the beginning, and second, the spiritual dimension of the tale as a whole, which has many aspects but is fundamentally about "mortifying" and ultimately transcending the body, or, as we are told near the end, about how to "raise the dead," which also means to "become spirit." Third, the narrator ascends and descends many times in the story and ultimately reaches a point near the end when he sees "one with a sword in his hand" in the East, another holding a bright disk, the "meridian of the Sun," and is told "The Work is completed." Finally, the tale is about sleeping, waking, breathing, dreaming, natural processes, and progress toward illumination.

But what are we to make of this enigmatic and seemingly inexhaustible vision as a whole? It definitely refers to working with plants and metals and mentions transmutation from a man of copper to a man of silver to a man of gold. It is about mortification and sacrifice and withstanding the "terrible mysteries" and about a "man of lead," "eyes full of blood," who is subjected to "an intolerable force." It is about the "art of the metals," we are told.

Yet it is also, simultaneously, spiritual. Later in this ur-text of Western alchemy, we see Agathodaemon, "an old man of hair so white that it is blinding," who, turning, gazed at the narrator "for an hour." Who is Agathodaemon? In ancient Greek tradition, drawing on ancient Egyptian religion, Agathodaemon (whose name means "good daemon") represented the goodness of life, fertility (including that of vineyards and crops), richness, and light and is associated with Helios (the Sun), with the serpent, and with the protection of the household and in at least one case, protection of a city (Alexandria). Invoking

Agathodaemon before a meal or toast is to invoke good spirits, light, and the brightness of the Sun.

What does it mean that Agathodaemon gazed at the narrator for an hour? And what does it mean that he is represented by an old man with blinding white hair? We may find our answer in the ancient Hermetic texts, the *Corpus Hermeticum 1*, where the narrator there tells us that he had a vision in which everything was light, "clear and joyful," and in seeing the vision he "came to love it." "I became transported as I gazed," he said. This vision of light is guided by the "master of all," the "man-shepherd," who reveals to him the true nature of things. And in the Hermetic account, as in Zosimos's, guided by an ancient elder, in vision the narrator sees a transporting vision of light, clarity, and joy. This is the terrible divine light that pervades nature, revealed by the "man-shepherd" who "gazed long into my eyes, so that I trembled."

In both cases, the narrator gazes into the terrible eyes of a divine guide, who is consciousness reflecting back upon itself, blinding in its light. The guide is the narrator's divine guide, revealing what is always present and beyond time or self, manifesting as pure, blinding radiance. Revealed to the narrator is that which is before the beginning and without end, out of which the panoply of nature ceaselessly emerges. The swirl of nature manifests within or from this radiance, divine light and life itself. In Zosimos's account, it lasts for an hour, not a flash, or a moment—it is an extended revelation, leading in turn to the enduring revelation of waking up to the divine Sun that can "make the eyes clear, and raise up the dead."

Here, in these ancient texts, we are called to ascend the steps of light, but beyond that, to encounter light. Encountering light is to encounter the hidden transcendent dimension within and beyond nature, and to encounter it is to be transformed. We must undergo an alchemical process of transmutation. In the ancient Hermetic text, the *Poimandres*, this process is described as an ascent through seven zones. In each zone we leave behind successive layers of selfishness, greed and anger, attraction and aversion, as well as ignorance (ensnaring falsehood), until finally we arrive at the eighth zone, which is free from these and full of joy. This eighth realm is gnosis, or divine realization.

So we are given the map of the terrain as a whole. But where are we now? Like Zosimos's narrator in his visions, we are in the nigredo, or black, phase—the phase of the dark, as discussed in chapter 1. We are at the beginning of the Work and must, like our narrator's visionary figures, undergo mortification. What is mortification? It is dying to our old self, or the dying away of our false self. To mortify is to die in order to truly live.

DYING TO OUR OLD SELF

There are different ways to understand this dying to or the dying of our old self. Of course, one is individual. But even at the individual level, can we really speak of our individual selves in isolation from our society? If we are in a dark age, then what role does that play in how we understand ourselves, others in society, and our world as a whole? We are born into a society, into a community, into particular families, among particular friends and acquaintances, and all of these form how we perceive everything around us. A dark age of dualistic materialism is pervasive, affecting everyone.

But we wake up individually, one by one. Zosimos also ascends the steps of light one by one. In his vision, he ascends steps of light into the light, but he does not do this only once. He ascends and descends, only to ascend again. The process is not a one-time affair but happens over and over, until finally he experiences a culmination and is told that the Work is completed.

Of course, Zosimos's vision is individual to him, in the sense that *he* ascends the steps of light, but the process also includes a vision of others and involves a series of "mortifications," the Latin root of which is *mort*, which means "dying" and connotes asceticism, a progressive dying to or of one's old self or outward identity, and the realizing of a new way of light-being in the world. But the path from darkness to illumination is not easy. It entails getting lost, being consumed by flames, and being cut up into pieces. The process described by Zosimos is grisly.

How can we understand Zosimos's alchemical process in relation to a society gone astray? One way is to see it as a process of leaving behind mistaken ideas of who we are and how we are in relation to the world, and of course this can be quite difficult. In traditional shamanism, the prospective shaman hears a call to separate himself from society, and at some point undergoes a breaking apart, a mortification, or a shattering of his old self so that a new shamanic self can come into being. In this process, the shaman leaves behind the old social identity and enters into a new way of being and acting in spiritual reality.

This separation from society is implied in Zosimos's visionary journey, and it is well known as an aspect of the traditional shamanic journey. A traditional shamanic culture is in principle supportive of the shamanic path, and still the shaman must heed a call to go outside it. How much more is such a separation process necessary in a materialistic, dualistic society built around belief systems that reject or denigrate spirituality and the spiritual path or that seek to convert it into a commercial enterprise? An authentic transformative spiritual path in such a society is even more challenging and perilous, isn't it?

You can learn to recognize the signs that mark opposition to your path, those who denigrate or reject the alchemical path of light, who tell you it's not "orthodox," or not "ideologically valid," or won't make you money—whatever objections and denigrations they raise. However they seek to "mortify" you, by such signs you will know them. Zosimos isn't telling you the path is easy. Quite the opposite. And even more so in a society that by and large doesn't support it but rather is based on premises fundamentally antithetical to it.

The truth is, the alchemical path is not for everyone. It is for those who heed an inner call to it. The idea of a dark age refers only to human society; in fact, it's quite possible that nature might thrive during a societal dark age and, for that matter, that spiritual life might flourish too. This flourishing begins individually and can happen regardless of what is occurring on a broader social scale. It is a call of the heart to light. Alchemy is transmutation—foremost, of us.

But this book goes beyond the personal or the individual. It includes the possibility of an alchemical community. Such a community is especially important during a dark age, since it represents an outpost of light. In fact, it is the future manifesting in the present.

The alchemical process can be understood as a map; one that can orient us in the particular terrain in which we find ourselves. Alchemical transformation can exist within different religious contexts—Christian, yes, but also Pagan, Hindu, and Buddhist, as all of these have highly developed alchemical traditions. Here, we're drawing primarily on the Western European alchemical tradition in order to discuss this process, but later we will reflect on how it can be manifested in particular places and among particular people, for it is ultimately a decentralized way of understanding how to live authentically and prosper.

THE ONE

In the *Emerald Tablet*, we are told that all things come from the mediation of the One, so all is born from the One. But what is this One? Plotinus* writes that the One is prior to and beyond being or multiplicity, prior also then to human intellect, and without any form. The One is not something that can be identified or identified with anything because it is prior to all differentiation. Humans have intellect, and our intellection reflects and derives from the One. Thus we can recognize the One through contemplation because the One is within us, and indeed, as the One, it has to be within us as well as within all beings.

---

*Plotinus (205–270 CE) was a great Platonic philosopher, who may have been born in Roman Egypt, and who developed his philosophical understanding in Alexandria under the tutelage of Ammonius Saccas, with whom Plotinus stayed for eleven years. He developed his philosophical circle in Rome, and his extraordinary collection of treatises, known as *The Enneads*, were compiled and organized by Porphyry, himself a great philosopher.

In Plotinus's work we see philosophy understood not as dry rationalistic treatises but as spiritual inquiry and record. Stephen MacKenna's translation of *The Enneads*, titled *Plotinus: The Enneads*, is considered beautiful for its prose, but any edition, especially the one from the Loeb Classical Library, will repay your perusal of it manyfold. I have spent some years reading primarily Plotinus.

Plato said in his "Seventh Letter" and Plotinus reiterated that seeing or recognizing the One is neither to be spoken nor written of. And yet it is possible, Plotinus continues, to point toward recognizing it, and the closer one ascends to seeing the One, the more one is illuminated in proximity to it, even if we are held back by our mundane concerns or impediments. Although it may be obscured, still, the One illuminates us to the extent we approach it in contemplation (*The Enneads* 6.9.3).

The One is prior to and within all being, and it is simple. It is the primal source out of which all emerges, and though all emerges from it, it is not diminished thereby. It is not created nor is it dependent on anything causal or contingent because it is prior to and beyond what is created, causal, or contingent (*The Enneads* 6.9.6). It is outside nothing, but is in all things. And when one approaches and bathes in the light of the One, then one becomes weightless, buoyant, and Plotinus tells us, "full of intellectual light," or rather, he continues, one becomes "pure light itself." Anyone who has seen it, Plotinus says, "knows what I mean" (*The Enneads* 6.9.9).

THE ALCHEMICAL QUEST FOR RESTORATION, TRANSFORMATION, AND ILLUMINATION

Although we are primarily drawing on Western alchemy, there are Indian and Tibetan traditions of alchemy that are woven into the stories of the *mahasiddhas*, the great transformative masters of Tibetan Buddhism. One famous mahasiddha known for alchemy was named Nagarjuna. Of course, the most famous Nagarjuna was renowned as the "second Buddha" because what he taught, the Madhyamika philosophical tradition, was so profound.

The other Nagarjuna was known as a great tantric master and disciple of the mahasiddha master Saraha and, through his practice of mantra and meditation, he became such an accomplished alchemist that he was capable of turning an entire mountain from iron into copper and then gold, though he refrained from the last because he was told so much gold in the end would be harmful to people.

One day, Nagarjuna met a herdsman who helped him cross a river, and as a reward for the herdsman's kindness, Nagarjuna granted his request to become a king. Thus the herdsman became known as King Shalabandha, and he ruled over eight million households. During his reign—which was prolonged by the alchemy of longevity that he had been taught by Nagarjuna—nature and humanity both flourished for a hundred years.

In this story of the mahasiddha called "Nagarjuna the Alchemist," we see that alchemy can be understood to be not only about individual transformation and recognition of the light, or the One, but also about *cultural* transmutation and illumination. For after King Shalabandha was taught the alchemy of immortality by Nagarjuna, his entire kingdom, including the land, plants, and animals, was blessed during his century-long reign. Alchemical transmutation of a whole locale or a region is possible in the context of profound spiritual realization, this Tibetan Buddhist legend tells us.

Here, as in the mythic Grail cycle, we see not only an illuminated sage, but also a renewed kingdom. Such a kingdom is limited in scope and time, it is true. But it has its day. It can exist. And for that time, an illuminated alchemical kingdom is possible, the stories tell us. But how? How do we get from a fallen age to an illumined sage or a regenerated kingdom?

We have to begin, as the Grail hero Parzival does, by asking the question, What ails us? What is wrong? Not superficially, but in a profound way. What has gone wrong, and how can things be restored? We are on a quest for ourselves, true, but also on behalf of others.

Ultimately, we are on a shared quest for the restoration of the kingdom and for illumination.

The quest begins with breaking through—we break through the falsehoods, through what my alchemist friend refers to as our "astrayness," and this allows us to go on our quest. We have to break through in order to start. And this breaking-through means we are called to go outside conventional social structures. We are called into the wild, into the realm of dreams and visions, poetry and song. And we heed our call.

Before there is community, there must be solitude for the quester. This is the individual path, that of the hermit, the recluse, the knight out on the sacred quest. You go out into the wild, on your own, and undergo a test, a time of learning and deepening, so that when you return—if you return—you do so as someone who understands his or her life path. We know we have a calling, but we must go on a quest to realize and fully understand it.

All things are born from the One into multiplicity, the *Emerald Tablet* tells us, and from this multiplicity we are called to return to the One. We make this journey first of all alone, as the individual quester who begins to realize that there is a path and that we can follow it. We begin to realize that we have a calling and that we can realize our calling. We can move from separation toward reunion. This breaking-through is a vital step on the path of light.

So what prevents us from knowing what our individual calling is? We could call it an astral shell.

3
The Astral Shell

Its father is the Sun, its mother is the Moon.
EMERALD TABLET

Although we typically are not aware of it, when we are born into a particular place and time, we live under a kind of mental carapace. This carapace is a social phenomenon unique to us as humans. Ultimately, it is illusory; it is sustained by our belief and participation in its apparent existence. It prevents us from seeing things as they really are. We are surrounded and inculcated from birth with social conditioning, so that we see the world as objects that we either want for ourselves or fear. In a technological world, this attraction-or-aversion existence is reinforced and amplified to a degree never before imagined, but the fundamentals remain the same. It's just that challenges in a technological society, to say nothing of a combined technological and ideological system, are much greater.

People who have awakened, in a social sense, are those who have recognized what I am referring to here and have made the effort to break free from the conditioning. As they do, they become internally independent of the collective system—they are beginning to wake up. Waking up is becoming aware of the ideological belief system imposed through governmental force, social censure, or all the other propaganda means, and refusing to accept it any longer.

Question: From what premises are you awakening? Answer: Materialistic ones. The word *materialistic* here means not so much the desire for and acquisition of objects, like a fine home or vehicle, as the underlying and erroneous belief that material reality alone exists. Those who see themselves as working with light already have left behind strictly materialistic premises. Not completely, but to at least some extent.

CONDITIONING IN A MATERIALISTIC SOCIETY

Often people assume that conditioning refers to traditional cultures or ways of being, and that a machine society or materialistic mass society represents freedom from conditioning, but the opposite is true. Let's consider a couple of examples. In a northern shamanic culture, society is organized around the partial transcendence of conditioning through shamanism, and in Tibetan Buddhist culture, it is organized around the complete transcendence of conditioning through meditation, ritual, and other practices. In other words, these traditional cultures were organized around paths to cosmological or metaphysical gnosis, a clear path beyond contingent social conditioning.

Gnosis (spiritual awakening) can be understood in terms of a spectrum from above to below. At the top is non-dual transcendent realization. Below that is realization of the One or unity of all things. Below that is cosmological gnosis, or insight into the hidden aspects of the cosmos, which is the underlying basis for magical or ritual practices that depend upon invisible connections between human, natural, and spiritual realms. Insight at any of these levels is a kind of gnosis. A culture expresses and is oriented toward cosmological and metaphysical gnosis—that is, toward spiritual awakening and liberation.

By contrast, a materialistic, technological mass society forms a kind of conditioning unknown in traditional cultures. This new conditioning is built into educational systems and manifests in production systems that include advertising, governmental administrative, legislative, and judicial elements, and even quasi-religious ideological aspects of civil society, in ways that don't exist at all in traditional cultures. The entire systemic edifice of technological mass society is built from materialistic and dualistic premises. It is about the celebration and gratification of the individual, the exploitation of nature's "resources," the enforcement of ideological proclamations, and conditioning that includes only the complacent or complicit and that excludes and vilifies dissidents. In such a society, history is rewritten, and the world is seen and seeable only through the thick and limiting goggles it proffers.

Waking up in this context means beginning to realize that the system as a whole, far from being a great advance on the past, in fact poses our greatest immediate challenge precisely because it seems to be all-pervasive. We don't see its conditioning precisely because we are conditioned *not* to see it. It is all-pervasive—like water to a fish or air to us—but virtually invisible for that very reason. Occasionally, remarkable people come along who help us to see what is actually all around us. Their action takes place as a natural result of who they are, like a catalyst dropped into a solution that suddenly turns it a color so we can see clearly in a new way.

Such moments of sudden clarification happen in a free environment, even if it's clandestine or explicitly outlawed. Someone, in a space of freedom, points out that such-and-such historical events did not really happen or did not happen that way, and from that prompting, or from the realization of such-and-such a politician's corruption, we begin to draw larger conclusions and eventually realize that even more was hidden from us than we initially realized. At some point, we might even begin to question the underlying premises of the materialistic system as a whole, including many of its nominally secular or religious critics presenting alternatives.

As early as the seventeenth and eighteenth centuries in Western Europe, there were some who recognized the role and nature of our collective conditioning, which existed already in confessional Protestant or Catholic Christian contexts. In that period, great mystics, such as before-mentioned Jacob Böhme, pointed out that just going to a "stone church," and adhering to putatively Christian social structures, actually can divert us from our true path, which is not dependent on outward social appearances but on our inner spiritual awakening and illumination. Those who insist on materialistic and dualistic premises and the views they inculcate keep us from waking up.

Metaphorically, adepts in this earlier era referred to some aspects of this carapace phenomenon as "the spirit of this world," meaning that which keeps us addicted to reactivity toward phenomena. In several traditions I'm familiar with, there are said to be entities or beings that draw from the more extreme manifestations of dualism and reactivity. Many nonphysical entities are understood to exist, some of which are seen as drawing energy from human warfare or mass movements. The "spirit of this world" more generally seeks to keep us captive, to lure us into temptation—that is, variants of attraction and aversion, and the more extreme the better.

The first step is realizing that what you have been conditioned with since you were little is often misleading or downright false, while the truth is kept hidden. This is hard for most people to grasp, depending on how deep the social conditioning inculcation has penetrated. What's more, often you need to go through this on your own, so it's easy to doubt yourself and take wrong turns. But it begins with a gut instinct, an inner knowledge that the system is deceptive and that there is a goal at the end of your quest. That goal is truth. You know that truth exists, and that it is key. This is the North Star or guiding light of your quest.

Part of this quest may be instinctively going into the wild, into nature. You may have felt a call toward solitude in wilderness or in closeness to nature, to water, earth, forest, mountains, and sky. Let us have a look at the epigraph quotation from the *Emerald Tablet* at the beginning of this chapter. What does this mean? "Its father is the Sun, its mother is the Moon. The wind carries it in its belly; the earth nourishes it." What does nature nourish in us and beyond us? What role does nature have in one's waking up?

When we are in large cities and constantly among other people, we are caught up in a kind of invisible collective climate zone. Even if we go into a park, and there are trees, perhaps a few birds or squirrels, still it is in the midst of the megalopolis. Of course, the wind and the waters and the earth exist here too, but it is hard for us to experience them deeply—how could we, amid city lights and the constant buzz?

A technological world is amplified by the media in general—especially social media—yet not everyone who participates in this invisible collective climate zone is consciously aware of its power. Of course, such a zone can manifest in many different ways. Another is ideological. In such a society, one's consciousness is bombarded with ideological conditioning from every direction and from many sources, including advertising, all news from controlled news sources, all levels of education beginning with primary school, all controlled publications, all publicly available, censored forms of social media, and so forth. Again, many people do not realize that they are surrounded by a constant cloud of propaganda. But some do, and many of them may want to free themselves from its influence.

BREAKING OUT OF THE CARAPACE OF CONDITIONING

If you feel yourself to be one of those seeking freedom from a collective climate zone or an ideological cloud, essentially, your path at this point begins with a kind of active detoxing. How do you detoxify yourself from these kinds of conditioning? Of course, you need to diminish their presence in your life as much as possible. To the extent you can, stop them at the source. If you can avoid it, don't spend time around people who believe in and repeat the propaganda. Seek out those who have become at least somewhat immune to it.

But there is more to do. It is not only a matter of getting out of the city into nature and finding kindred spirits, though these are vital. There is also an individual process to engage in, and being in natural surroundings among those of like mind is conducive to that process. This is the alchemical process that this book introduces and encourages. This process is alluded to in the *Emerald Tablet* with the assertion that "its father is the Sun, its mother is the Moon."

The Sun and the Moon are not only external objects in this tradition; they are also inner principles that infuse the natural world and us. There is an inner process where the solar masculine and lunar feminine principle combine. But to engage in this process, you must first have broken free of the materialistic premises that are so deeply embedded in machine-society, and have created space in your life for the process.

Breaking out of the carapace, or astral shell, of materialism is the beginning because otherwise you are caught in the false, artificial realm of human-generated social illusions. And this realm of socially generated illusions (really, we can call them what they are—deceit and lies) is only intensified and made to seem more real by technology. Virtual reality, artificial intelligence, games—all the machinery magical in its technological sophistication—distract you from this alchemical process and from working with light and the inner principles.

This is why this is a path not for the many but for the few. It appeals to those who hear its call; for those who do not, it is as if it does not exist at all. Those who do not hear the call are conditioned their whole lives not to hear it. They are not the ones reading these lines of prose. Or if they are reading them, they cannot hear or resonate with what is being said. That lack of resonance is what we refer to as the astral shell. The call, then, is not for them. It is for you, if you hear it, and for those like you.

When we look back at the history of the West and the most archaic and profound traditions of the West, we can see opposition to those traditions playing out in different ways. It is not, as some think, only a matter of modern materialism being opposed to the inner alchemical path. The opposition to spiritual awakening in the West goes far back and is found in the history of monotheisms (religions that believe that only one God exists), which really are monolatries (religions that worship a single god or egregore but do not necessarily deny the existence of others). When a deity commands, or is purported to command, the tearing down of the sacred trees or monuments of other traditions and the total destruction of others' culture and population, when a bureaucratic apparatus is established to annihilate "Pagans" or "heretic" mystics, fundamentally, these manifest opposition to the integrated alchemical transformative path we are discussing throughout this book.

In other words, although we do not need to dwell on it, we should recognize that there is a long history of what we are referring to as an astral shell, a stubbornly dualistic perspective tied to a materialistic worldview dogmatically imposed on others. Such a perspective cannot abide what we are discussing in this book, and it manifests itself in putatively secular academia as well, which is largely an extension of early monotheistic forms of asserted dominance and proscription transposed into a virulently ideological pseudo-religious state-enforced system.

Whose father is the Sun and mother the Moon? The alchemical child. This can be understood as a different way of describing what we are calling breaking through the carapace, a way of describing waking up to reality beyond the social illusions. This process of waking up takes place in phases, in levels or degrees. The alchemical path is one of being born again, or reborn, a process of rebirth, growth, and maturity. It also can be understood as an infant or child who is conceived, born, and is growing up. We are that child.

Breaking through the carapace is moving from the black stage of the process (nigredo) to the white stage (*albedo/candeo*): from darkness into light. The black stage is the condition of darkness, of being benighted, caught in emotional reactivity. The nigredo also can be self-righteousness—one's own self-important certitude means one condemns what is actually the truth, but one doesn't recognize it. Materialistic dualism means self-righteously rejecting what is true on false premises, but of course, we don't recognize such premises as false because the entire system around us is built to manifest and enforce them.

Essentially, what we're discussing here is a process of being reborn, of waking up, which also means giving up a world of lies and propaganda or false premises that many not only take for granted but in fact seek to self-righteously impose on others. Such is the opposite of the natural way that is the alchemical process. This process is not exclusive to any organized religion, even though it can be found, for instance, in the Christian Mysteries, if we understand Christ as the revealer of light and of the light's mysteries. Still, it is a process of nature herself, and natural to us as human beings.

This is the beauty of the alchemical tradition, whose roots go far back into the archaic Eurasian tradition: it draws on the language of nature to express a process and truths that we can all understand and realize for ourselves. It also expresses the basis not only for our own individual renewal but also for a larger, decentralized, and profound cultural renewal. But all this is predicated on entering into a new path, and to do that we need to begin by breaking free of conditioning, by realizing that there *is* a new path and that we need to embark upon the journey of traveling it. As more people share this realization, new communities will begin to appear.

For new communities and germinal cultures to emerge first of all requires individuals and small groups to awaken. Sometimes you may read about an envisaged "new age" dawning without requiring any waking up and the travails that go along with it. The hard work of waking up is imagined to be replaced by a collective dimensional shift, or a magical date, which owes more than a little to the earlier belief in many envisaged but erroneous dates for the return of Christ and a millennial era on Earth. A new age is a secular version of Christian millenarianism, and they both serve to externalize our expectations and thus to distract us from engaging in our own and shared alchemical process of illumination.

What adepts referred to as the astral shell can also be termed "conditioning," or "preconceptions," but it goes beyond these because it includes both our individual and collective barriers to waking up. One way to understand waking up is as piercing through the astral shell that appears to block us from the light. In this process, we first must recognize that there is a path and a goal and that we can realize that goal by walking the path. Knowing this is not the same as accomplishing it, but it is a necessary beginning. If we are going to a destination, first we must know the destination is there.

Then, on our path, we encounter others, and they in turn can support and help us just as we can help them in our shared progress. That is alchemical community. A community can be scattered, of course, but ultimately, it also needs to be in a particular place, for only then can we develop a harmonic relationship between the community, nature as manifested in that place, and spirit. Whether alone or with others, we each must begin to recognize the burdens we carry, and how to lay them down and transmute ourselves and the place where we are.

Once you break out of the shell of materialism, you can begin to engage in the process that the *Emerald Tablet* refers to with the phrase "its father is the Sun, its mother is the Moon." Our inner solar masculine and lunar feminine principles appear to be separated but in fact are complementary and ultimately are united in the One. The path of light, in a couple, illuminates our masculine and feminine natures that, when joined, ultimately form a union in eternity. But to accomplish this union, we must begin to shed the burdens we carry.

4
The Burdens We Carry

The wind carries it in its belly; the earth nourishes it.
EMERALD TABLET

The alchemical path is conveyed with symbols and metaphors. It is not that there is literally an astral shell. Rather, the astral shell is a symbol, conveying a certain psychic and spiritual way of understanding our predicament. Likewise, it is not that we literally are carrying burdens, like a suitcase, or a weighted yoke. Rather, this too is a symbolic way of expressing a truth about ourselves. What is it that keeps us in our same unhealthy habits, that prevents us from realizing fully who we are and flourishing? What is wrong with us or awry in our lives that makes us continue in the same dysfunctional patterns despite ourselves? On some level, we know.

THE BURDENS WE CARRY

We are human pack animals, weighed down with all the baggage we carry. Who has burdened us? Of course, we inherit baggage, not only personally, from our families, but also generationally and socially, from society as a whole. Many of these generational and social burdens are actually lies presented as truth, but if we are immersed in the system, we won't recognize this. How could we? We need a reference point from outside the system in order to see. We can call finding that vantage point piercing the astral shell.

But even dimly beginning to recognize from this new perspective that we are burdened means that we can continue to grow. There is a little light, where before there was just darkness. In darkness, we can't see, but when there is a little light, we can begin to make out what before we could not, and this in itself is a major breakthrough. We begin to recognize that so much of what is taken for granted in society is mistaken or misleading. Material reality is not the only reality. Spiritual life is not just belief.

We begin to see through the social façade. We begin to see the burdens we carry as different kinds of baggage. Some are valises or trunks we've never even looked inside but have carried along for generations, others are more familiar to us, and a few are definitely our own. Generational baggage includes that of your people and their history, as well as the prevailing views and social system shared by others, including also those of other peoples that intersect with our own in some ways. This is collective, shared, not only individual, but we forget that we participate in it, conditioned, as we well may be, that our "individual" identity is all that matters.

We are subject to the vast forces of history, the sweep of social systems, conditioning from educational systems and government and corporate propaganda, and advertising, much of which is akin to the air surrounding us that we also do not see. And we are subject to generational forces, to patterns passed down through tribes and families that can gather strength as they are reinforced unconsciously by previous generations, by those around us, even by us. In some cases, these forces can take on a kind of semi-autonomy as a kind of tribal-familial entity, sometimes referred to as an egregore.

An egregore might be presented or regarded as a god, but in reality it is a very particular kind of collectively generated and reinforced entity, usually temporary, though possibly long-lived, that requires the continuous attention and intentional contributions of its adherents and that in turn may be able to grant worldly boons. We see something like such entities manifest through public spectacles such as sports and politics, as well as in some religious phenomena. It feeds on public attention, and it may in some cases be associated by adherents with luck or good fortune in worldly endeavors.

A term like *egregore* is a way of expressing metaphorically a kind of addictive psychological power that affects many people, not just us. It is a way of describing a collectively produced and reinforced entity or kind of consciousness that may be difficult for us to recognize on our own, and that even then may seem difficult to gain freedom from. But once we have understood the concept, we can begin to apply it and to see how it operates in the world around us, as well as how we can free ourselves from its hold.

Of course, societal, generational, and familial baggage is not something we can or need to erase, even if that were possible. Social forces, systemic propaganda, and generational and familial patterns all are beyond us as individuals, with causes that go far back in time and that obviously affect or entrap many people, not only us. We can point this out to others, but whether they will listen is another matter. What we *can* do, and indeed, what we *must* do, is move toward greater consciousness, greater awareness that these forces and patterns exist, which also moves us toward greater freedom.

Modern technological society is filled with addictions and distractions. In fact, much technology functions as a combination of addiction and distraction—it's not as though we can remove these elements. They're woven into its very nature. Games, virtual reality, social media feeds, and online "hits" all are *designed* to suck us in and keep us immersed in them. Technological distractions are inherently addictive—they're *intended* to be that way. Woven into this distractive and addictive media is larger social programming. Ideology, propaganda, distraction, addiction, fearmongering . . . all of these work to keep us in the dark in different but coordinated ways. These are also the burdens we carry.

All these elements, which are both outside and inside us, are interwoven with our own habitual patterns. Angry, jealous, spiteful, greedy, prideful, thoughtless patterns, along with the wrongs we've done, our mistakes, and our foolishness are all embedded in us through repetition. And there are the interpersonal dynamics that reinforce such behavior, with our partner, with our siblings or parents, with friends, or with coworkers. Perhaps we're not aware of such dynamics at all—or perhaps we are only dimly aware and feel powerless to stop ourselves from lashing out or taking some other impulsive action. All these are burdens we carry.

We can lay our burdens down. We may or may not be able to convince others, or to affect their journeys, but we definitely can undertake our own journey from entrapment toward freedom. The first step is to realize that these burdens exist, and that we carry them along with us, remaining unconscious of them and their power over us. We have dualism and materialism inculcated into how we see the world, while spiritual dimensions of life are ignored and denigrated. We are embedded in familial dramas; we are caught in all-too-familiar patterns. But nonetheless, at some point, we began to awaken; we began to glimpse light, and then, in time, to move toward it. This is the process of laying our burdens down.

How do we do this? By turning our attention to the light within. The dark is very familiar to us, and so the light, any light, is a little unusual. This is why we practice becoming familiar with the light.

THE ALCHEMICAL PATH OF LIGHT

A friend of mine who has worked with the alchemy of light for many years reminds us that by putting our attention on the light, by relaxing into the light, we are becoming more and more familiar with it, and it is the light, he says, that unburdens us. Gradually, it dissolves our fears, attachments, anger, and anxieties. We acclimate ourselves to it.

In the ancient Mysteries, the initiates would go into darkness and experience intense emotional suffering. They would experience fear and being lost in the darkness. Then they would experience the light in the darkness, the great joy and illumination of freedom. This light was also immortal, beyond the vicissitudes of mortal attachments and aversions, beyond time, as I discussed in *Entering the Mysteries*. They experienced paradise, and because they experienced it for themselves while alive, they would experience paradise after death.

Alchemical lightwork can be Pagan, as the ancient Mysteries were, or it can be Christian, because Christianity also can be understood as a mystery religion. The alchemical path does not belong only to one religious tradition. It is an individual path of awakening, a symbolic way of understanding that is fundamentally human and can be understood in terms of the ancient Mysteries, Platonism, Christianity, Buddhism, and other religious traditions. It provides an entryway and guide to the path of illumination, but we must each walk the path ourselves.

Of course, the alchemical path means understanding Christianity, for instance, in new ways. The alchemical path illuminates what otherwise remains hidden in Christianity. Christ's harrowing of hell, Christ as lightbringer, Christ as the Sun, Christ as the revealer of mysteries and initiator into eternal life . . . these are all there in Christianity, but we see them more clearly with the aid of the alchemical path. Invoking Christ awakens the light in us so that we can gradually overcome and be free from the burdens we once carried.

It might seem we can pursue the alchemical path on its own, to some extent, without reference to a particular tradition. We can rest our attention on the light and allow it to gradually dissolve our burdens. After all, the reason the alchemical path can appear in different religious forms is that it reflects fundamental truths about who we are, and how we can become better and wiser human beings. These truths are not a matter of opinion but rather are inherent in who we are, and we can each discover them for ourselves.

If this is so, you might ask, Why would we need a particular religious tradition? Why should alchemy incorporate particular religious symbols, like an image of the resurrected Christ? The answer is probably not what you think. The answer is because finding and staying on the path of light is difficult for us because we are caught in the burdens we carry.

We are blocked by our preoccupations, our distractions and addictions, our habitual responses, our greed, jealousy, anger, and fear. Light from the other side reaches out toward us, but we must reach out toward it at the same time in order to make the connection, and revealed traditional religion helps us do that.

Each of us has individual burdens and a unique path to follow beyond them, but at the same time, light by its very nature illuminates, and that illumination is not ours alone. This is why in the famous Hermetic treatise *Poimandres*, we find a revealer figure by that name. The treatise begins with the narrator being beyond the bodily senses, when a vast being announces itself as a sovereign mind that is always present. This vast being in some sense then becomes the portal through which the narrator is able to see in infinite vision, light and joy, as well as darkness and the interactions of fire, air, and earth. Poimandres, the revealer, identifies himself as the light itself, and when the narrator looks him in the face, he sees immeasurable light powers. By the end of the treatise, the narrator is deeply happy and able to share the path of light with others because his mind was receptive to Poimandres, inspired by the sacred breath of truth itself, identical to the light.

We see also in the dream alchemy of Zosimos: there is a revealer figure of light in dialogue with the protagonist or narrator, a kind of syzygy, or outward manifestation of light, that the narrator experiences as an angelic or divine revealer-other, yet what is revealed is the narrator's own light-nature itself. This process of light revelation is depicted in visions or dreams—hence in a condensed way—but is almost certainly gradual for us as expressed in our daily lives, in the process of invoking the light, of becoming light.

We are, in a sense, in a dialogue with our own light-nature, seen as outside of us as our angelic light guide; not us, yet, in a profound sense, also us. This is what the *Poimandres* depicts. And of course we each experience this for ourselves in our dreams, when we see in our mind's eye ourselves and others who we experience as others, yet exist ultimately in our own mind, both "other" and "not other" at once.

The alchemical visionary texts we have been drawing on are like this—dreamlike—because this is how our mind naturally moves toward illumination, aided by light narratives with a revealer of light. The revealer may be Poimandres or Thrice-Great Hermes or Christ or Guru Rinpoche. It is through the revealer, the light within the darkness, that the darkness is overcome and vanquished utterly.

There may be a few very unusual people who are able to be illuminated at once, in one fell swoop like a bolt of lightning, but the alchemical path I was taught by a long-time practitioner is a lifetime process of invoking and allowing the light to gradually penetrate and illuminate our darkness, trauma, and negative emotion. This is not necessarily easy work. We have to face our own flaws, our weaknesses, our vanity, and our delusions. And of course we don't want to see these, but the light by its very nature illuminates them.

VANQUISHING THE DARKNESS

Bear in mind that we are not separate from the society in which we were born. It shapes us, and we may in our turn shape it for the future. But to shape the future, to help develop living culture, we must begin with ourselves and our own awakening. In the *Poimandres*, the narrator is able to share the light with others only after he has experienced it by looking into Poimandres's face of light. We must engage in illuminating our own darkness before we can assist in illuminating the darkness in others.

To talk about the darkness, you must refer to the light. Unburdening ourselves in this alchemical tradition does not happen on its own, as if there were some process of darkness in darkness, because darkness cannot transform darkness, nor can it illuminate anything. Only the light can illuminate darkness, and if full light is thrown upon darkness, as we all know, the darkness vanishes instantly as if it was never there in the first place.

In a real sense, we live in a dark age. What is a dark age? It is a materialistic, antispiritual, nihilistic time. A time when knowledge is outlawed, willful ignorance is empowered, and centralized, spiteful, and unilateral power is wielded against dissidents, while those in power enrich themselves. It is a time of cultural disintegration, of wisdom being derided while folly is extolled and held up as a standard for all.

And yet . . . we know instinctively that the darkness cannot long be sustained, for light vanquishes darkness. The burdens we carry are in one sense real and, in another, an illusion. They are real so long as the darkness endures, and yet in the brilliance of light, there is no darkness, there are no burdens. Both can be true. And even in a dark age, one where materialism and nihilism are fiercely asserted to be true, as soon as there is light, they fade and vanish as if they, like the darkness, never were there at all.

The *Emerald Tablet* refers to the wind carrying it in its belly, and the earth nourishing it. "It" is the inherent life energy in our belly—it is what nourishes and grounds us. As we begin to lay down our burdens, the natural life energy of our *hara*, or the region around and below the navel, begins to strengthen. Moving through the black stage into the white, into illumination, means allowing nature's inherent energy to manifest in and around us. We let go of the burdens we carry and begin to join with life in a new way. We experience a rebirth.

So our vision is what sustains us through a dark age and what will dawn on the other side. It preserves and encourages the signs that point toward the light, that remind us of the light, of how to be caretakers of the great records, the signs of the eternal. The alchemical process entails recognizing the individual, family, and collective burdens we carry and allowing those to be illuminated so that we can be transformed through that illumination. Because you are reading these words, you have already begun this natural and sublime process. In the next chapter, we will begin to explore the essence of this process—light, illumination.

— PART TWO —
THE WHITE

5
The Light of Nature

It causes works of wonder (telesmi) and is the completion of the whole world.

EMERALD TABLET

It is no accident that traditions of both East and West refer to enlightenment, or illumination. As we discussed throughout part one, light is the central metaphor for spiritual awakening. But is it a metaphor? What is the role of light? What is its meaning? What does it mean to refer, as the alchemist Thomas Vaughan did, to the light of nature (*lumen naturae*) or to the essential role of light in the alchemical process? Finally, to what is the *Emerald Tablet* referring with "works of wonder" and "the completion of the whole world"? Here we find keys to the Western Mysteries and, in particular, to continuity of the ancient collective Mysteries with the more individualized alchemy and the alchemical process.

What is the white stage in our journey? It is purification, which also means the light breaking out in and over our darkness, illuminating us and the world around us. In the white stage, we begin to see that light is present in nature around us, and that we have greater capacity to perceive and to radiate that light than we previously knew. It is the time in our journey when we begin not only to see more deeply into our own nature, but also into nature and nature's hidden dimensions.

The alchemist Thomas Vaughan, in his treatise *Aula Lucis*, discusses the mysteries of light. The Latin word *aula* refers to the inner court or hall in the royal castle or palace, the place of royal power, and the word *lucis* means "light," so the title of his work, while often translated as "House of Light," also suggests the inner royal hall of light. Vaughan writes that he who seeks happiness must look after light, for there is the cause of happiness "both temporal and eternal." The house of light, he continues, is not hard to find because light itself "walks in before us and is the guide to his own habitation." Light is "the artist that shapes all things;" light is an inexhaustible treasure, blessed and raised above the Earth's circle; nature herself tells us that "our happiness consists in light."

The Sun is the light of all nature, as the ancient *Turba Philosophorum* puts it, without which all creatures would be darkened. But, the *Turba* continues, there is "a light more subtle and lucid than the light of the sun." Thus, it suggests, there are actually two kinds of light: the light by which we see and a more subtle and sublime light. Angels are more lucid than the Sun, Moon, and stars; theirs is a more subtle and sublime light, as they are divine emanations, closer to the divine than to the earthly.

How is light happiness? Vaughan presents us with an enigma. From an earthly perspective, the Sun is the source of light that makes crops grow and creatures flourish, and in this sense the Sun brings happiness. But Vaughan is not referring only to the Sun and to light we see. He is also referring to light that is an inexhaustible treasure, that blesses and raises us up or exalts us, that is the nature of angels, that infuses all things. This is a different order of light; this light is not only outer, but also inner.

THE LIGHT INSIDE US

The alchemical physician Paracelsus[*] referred to the light of nature but also to the divine light that is its ultimate source. These two are not in

---

[*]Paracelsus (1493–1541) was a Swiss physician and alchemist. A selection of his writings was edited by Nicholas Goodrick-Clarke in *Paracelsus: Essential Readings*, and another collection by Arthur Edward Waite, *The Hermetic and Alchemical Writings of Paracelsus*, was published and republished in different editions over the past century.

opposition, but rather the light of nature is a reflection of the supernal divine light; living in harmony with the light of nature, we invoke and immerse ourselves in the divine light. Alchemical spiritual practice is invoking and allowing ourselves to be immersed in the transcendent luminosity at the heart of nature and of us.

It is relatively easy, especially in an artificial society, to convince ourselves that we are alienated beings in an alien world, and with regard to technological, modern society, there is truth to this view. However, there is another perspective, one much more ancient and attuned to the mysteries of nature. This other perspective can be called Platonic or Neoplatonic or Hermetic, but here we use primarily the term *alchemical*. The alchemical understanding centers not on fallenness—though that exists—but on restoration or transmutation, on transfiguration and raising up, on the sublime.

Light is the heart of this alchemical process; it is our guide to its own habitation. Reality is not only materiality. Our own consciousness, should we consider it directly, tells us this by its very nature. Light enables us to see, to recognize, to understand. This is true in an earthly sense, of course—by day we see, by night in nature we are dependent on the light of the Moon and stars, and see less clearly. But it is also true metaphorically. Hence we refer to the "light dawning" in our mind's eye. We know that there is another kind of light, one more subtle in the province of our mind.

It is in this sense that we work with light. This light, Vaughan tells us, can transmute what it touches. As the "elect substance of heaven and earth," "it blesses us, providing an inexhaustible treasure" that rises up above the circle of Earth. This light is of a different order and is not only external in the material world; it is also an inner light that illuminates and completes at the same time. It is a light inside nature and also inside us. We see it in the green of tree leaves and needles, in the eyes of animals and fishes, in all of life, glowing from within. We see this light illuminating the paintings by the great artists of the Hudson River School; it is subtle and sublime; it raises us and our world up. It transfigures and transmutes.

But this light cannot be shut up in a box or a darkened room; it cannot be captured. It eludes us. We can only make a home for it, a "house of light." And what is that house of light? It is, Vaughan tells us, an "oily, ethereal substance" alone that retains it. And from this "oily, ethereal substance" we can "impart and communicate it to what bodies we please, giv[ing] the basest things a most precious luster and a complexion as lasting as the sun." Here Vaughan tells us that he is revealing the heart of the alchemical mysteries: "This is that mystery which the philosophers have delivered in [most obscure terms] . . . yet I do affirm . . . that this secret was never communicated to the world in a discourse so plain as this."

When we go into the wilderness, away from the human-centric urban sprawl of pavement and concrete and noise, we surround ourselves with and are imbued with life from the light of nature. Why do religious anchorites or hermits go into the wilderness to live? Of course, in part it is to be free from the hubbub of human society and its myriad addictions and temptations. But perhaps also it is because in nature we are restored because we are immersed in its special living light, imbued with it, and we become alive anew with it. On some level, we know this instinctively; we recognize the vital glint in the eye of the ruddy farmer or fisherman.

And there are other mysteries also in Vaughan's allusive comment. There is in us an "oily, ethereal substance" that we can communicate to other bodies as we wish, "giving the basest things a most precious luster and a complexion as lasting as the sun." What "basest things"? The inner light can transmute all that surrounds us in the natural world, so the most mundane details of an insect or a stone can be magical. But there is also a mystery of subtle communication between a man and a woman, or between friends, that imputes light and luster to life "as lasting as the sun."

The "oily, ethereal substance" to which Vaughan refers is akin to *ojas*, or life energy, in Ayurveda. We can enhance or diminish our life energy, depending on our activities, our food and drink, our sleep patterns, our time in nature and in the light of the Sun and the Moon, all the different aspects of our life that cause our life energy to wax or wane. And among the "basest things" is sexual activity which, after all, indeed can dissipate our vitality. But in some circumstances, it also can augment our life energy and imbue us with "a most precious luster" and a solar radiance. Life energy can be communicated to and with another. We recognize the presence of life intuitively in others, for some look haggard and dissipated, while others seem to radiate good health. When we are close to someone radiant, we feel a little more radiant ourselves.

Nature is the house of light, and we can bathe in that light. There is the light of the Sun, the light of the Moon, the light of the stars, and the light within nature and the Earth. We can bathe in the light of nature, consciously allowing the Sun's light upon us to be radiant within our solar plexus and abdomen—we can consciously be within the Earth, in a cave or an underground chamber, just as we can bathe in the starlight of the night sky. For, as R. J. Stewart has observed, there is a light in the Earth. Each of these is both an outward bathing and an inner knowing.

The *Emerald Tablet* alludes to how the heart of the mystery "causes works of wonder (*telesmi*) and is the completion of the whole world." To what is this referring? The works of wonder could be understood as magical or transmuting powers or abilities. The completion can be understood as initiation—to be initiated is to be purified by lustration and ultimately illuminated. The telesmatic Mysteries in ancient times were those that involved human *telos*, the fulfillment of what it means to be human, to become immortal, and to enter paradise. Transmuting the world through "telesmi" and "the completion of the whole world" refer to our becoming more fully realized, which has implications for this worldly life (telesmi, alchemical works of wonder), and for the afterlife (paradise).

Reflect on life lived in the light of nature. First, of course, individual life—you choose to live among trees and waters, growing and harvesting your own food, living in and with nature. Second, the life of the couple in the light of nature, each complementing and augmenting the other. Third, the life of the family in the light of nature. Fourth, community life in the light of nature. These four are all interwoven, integrated and integral to flourishing. From the individual to the community, all in a culture have a shared understanding, a shared communal and individual orientation and telos.

LIVING IN THE LIGHT OF NATURE

The alchemy of culture, or the alchemical culture, is an overarching theme of this book. The alchemical culture is transmutation of ourselves, others, and nature through illumination. Light pervades nature. Nature emerges from, bathes in, and returns to light. And when we are attuned to that light, we and nature both flourish. This is part (but not all) of what is meant by the "completion of the whole world."

What we conceive can manifest. This is true for the worst as well as for the best, which is how the most diabolical and destructive technologies came into existence. But instead of creating concrete and metal insect hives, why not turn to conceiving the best and most harmonious way of life attuned to the rhythms of nature and the spiritually aware? Why not envision life lived in the light of nature?

To do this is to develop community with a shared purpose and spiritual aim. Such a community's goals are fundamentally different from the aims of a materialistic and exploitative society. The flourishing of human culture, of nature, and of spirituality together forms a way of being in the world that is oriented toward cosmological and metaphysical gnosis. Such a culture is oriented toward human and natural flourishing and spiritual realization.

What does such a culture look like? It is adapted to a particular landscape and people. To live in the light of nature is to live with and in nature and to recognize that in it and around us are all manner of visible and invisible beings. Alchemical culture is a way of life integrated with the visible and invisible aspects of our world. What we are reflecting on here is how to create a path of life in the light of nature.

We need to understand that most of humanity, including most of the European diaspora, collectively took a path away from such a way of life. Going down a materialistic and dualistic secular path gave humanity great power to exploit and destroy, but we left behind our ancestral traditions and cultures and in so doing lost our way. It is always possible to begin anew. We can do so now; we can seed a future where conditions will make it inevitable for others also to be able to take this path in the light of nature.

Did we *have* to go through all the perfidy and destruction during the period often called "modernity"? Was it inevitable that there be vast wars and communist dictatorships and gulags and all the horrors that accompanied them? Did the agrarian foundation of society *have* to be thoroughly destroyed? To what extent did Catholicism and Protestantism give birth to secularism, materialism, scientism, and the atomization of the technological age? At some point, it may be worthwhile to consider such questions, and exactly how cultures around the world were obliterated in the span of a century or two, almost the blink of an eye in world time.

But here our eyes are on the future and on the emergence of illuminated cultures in which humanity, nature, and the spirit world can flourish together. This is not to idealize the past or the future—of course human beings are given to all manner of bad behavior. In Christianity, this is called humanity's fallen nature. But the very idea of fallen nature implies that it once was not fallen, that it need not be fallen, that it can be restored. Alchemy is the process of restoration, of a return to the primordial.

When we look at archaic cultures, whether in the Himalayas, in central Eurasia, or in Western Europe, we often find family crests marking ancestral connections to a particular guardian spirit in the form of a mythical creature, sometimes a bird of prey, sometimes a dragon or griffin, sometimes a wolf or another kind of animal. The main founding tribes of the upper Himalayas each were identified with a particular mythical animal. We see something similar in some American Indian tribes where ancestral totems take the form of mythical animals.

What does this totemic identification signify? Above all, a unity or synergy between the human cultural, animal, and spiritual realms. The ancestral totem links together all the realms, or put another way, it is an area at which all three intersect at the center of a triquetra. The ancestral totemic mythical animal signifies the emergence of a particular branch of the human cultural family from timelessness and the spirit into nature, and through nature into the culture. To bear it or to invoke it is to invoke not only the ancestors but also their and our timeless origin. There is mystery in this.

The phrase "light of nature" can be understood in multiple ways and on multiple levels, but at heart it expresses the intersection and union of spirit and nature. In an individual, it manifests as life force, vitality, and inexpressible but unmistakable radiance. In a community and in a region, too, it manifests more broadly in the same way. This inexpressible vitality and unity may be signified by a mythical totemic animal for individuals, families, tribes, cities, and regions. Each may have its signature guardians. The term *mythical* expresses the totems' timeless origin and nature; they could be understood as a signature link for a particular person, family, tribe, city, or region, between timelessness and time.

When we look at the diasporic movement of European settlers across North America, we see that while they had extraordinary fortitude and stoic will to endure and to prevail over enormous challenges, and indeed while they were remarkably successful in clearing land and making farms, roads, homes, stores, manufactories, and towns from wilderness, most brought with them a worldview devoid of anything we have been discussing in this chapter. As a result, most American settlers *overcame* but did not connect with or even acknowledge such ideas as spirits of nature or household spirits or profound connections between land, water, culture, and spirit realms in the place where they settled. Some did, of course, as they brought European folkways with them, as in Pennsylvania or the Appalachians. But many did not.

There is a distinctive spirit to place, a spiritual signature to be recognized and realized, and this is a task for emergent cultures. We can call this process deep rooting, the depths here being spiritual depths. There is, as R. J. Stewart points out, Earth light, a special kind of light of the cosmos itself within the Earth. We can experience this Earth light for ourselves through inner vision or perception. And there are particular qualities in and destinies for different continents and regions, which each have their own dispersed guardians and aspects that may take centuries to be recognized and manifested culturally. We need to understand that cultures emerge out of place; they are not imposed on it from without, but emerge from within the spiritual archetypes in particular configurations of earth, waters, and sky.

All this and more, we can term the light of nature. From it, the *Emerald Tablet* tells us, come telesmi, works of wonder, and the completion of the whole world. We glimpse supersensual or transcendent light through the light of nature. The light of nature is its manifestation in the world around us, the house of light. Our task is to realize this for ourselves, where we are.

6
Turning toward Earth

Its power is complete if it be turned toward earth.
EMERALD TABLET

When we undertake spiritual endeavors, we are not alone. We may believe we are alone, that our journey is only ours as an individual, and some encourage such a view, especially in the atomized era of individualism. We might think we are engaged in "self-help," and of course in some sense we are, but there is more to it than that. For when we genuinely are engaged in a spiritual path, we are not alone. Who is present with us?

First, there are those in the past, future, and present who have undertaken the spiritual journey, especially those who have left for us a symbolic record of reminders, suggestions, or advice and with whom we are through that medium, as through an invisible cord, connected. Of course, Zosimos, the authors of versions of the *Emerald Tablet*, Thrice-Great Hermes, and more recent authors like Thomas Vaughan, all belong, we think, in the past; we think they are caught in time as if in amber, frozen. But there is another way of knowing them, and we intuit this. For all who engage in the journey have as their companions others who in the past have engaged in the journey.

Second, there are our contemporary companions on the inner journey. This inner journey is the heart of authentic culture; culture is born from the journey and exists in order to encourage us on it. Regardless of how debased outward society appears to be, if there are others also on this journey, then there is an alternative culture already existent, comprised of our companions. Communities emerge naturally from the camaraderie of spiritual companionship.

Then there are our hidden companions. One group of hidden companions is from the past and can be found in books and manuscripts and images, texts signaling to us the inner path, its dangers, and its signposts on the way. In a dark age, it is critical that we have collections of such works. Some of us have been creating libraries and online resources that keep the flame alive and provide resources for pilgrims who seek the companionship of those who have undertaken the journey before them and know the way. These are like beacons, places lighted from within, beckoning us to enter.

Then there are the invisible companions, including those from the future, in some sense also present with us if we are on the journey. Many in the age of materialism see time as immutable, and of course it seems on the surface that the past is past, perpetually separated from the present and both separated from the future. But time's immutability is illusory; the closer we are to eternity, the more we see the truth of this. All who undertake the inner journey are in time and eternity, but drawing closer to eternity, or timelessness, and also therefore, to each other, regardless of disparate time or distance.

We have two kinds of ancestors. Of course, we have our genetic ancestors, our familial forefathers, and they are present with us. But then there is also our spiritual genealogy, our spiritual forefathers, and they too watch over, guide, and accompany us. What's more, our spiritual genealogy includes not only those in the past but also those in the present and future who share with us the alchemical journey. We are part of a vast community, both visible and invisible. The invisible portion is the larger by far.

TURNING THE POWER TOWARD EARTH

What does the *Emerald Tablet* mean when it says that "its power is complete if it be turned toward earth"? "Turned toward earth" can be understood as the transmutation of and in the natural world. This transmutation is sometimes described as the philosopher's stone, or in the Grail cycle, sometimes as the grailstone. Why stone? A stone is usually conceived of as inanimate, and in the modern materialistic view, as without life. From such a perspective, a stone is just an object. But neither the philosopher's stone nor is the grailstone is just an object. Rather, both are charged, the power of transmutation alive in the apparent solidity of the stone.

Many people assume that the Holy Grail is a cup, and it is described sometimes as a chalice. But it is also described as a grailstone and in terms that make it clear that it is not any ordinary stone, but rather, the philosopher's stone. The philosopher's stone is an ancient alchemical term for the power turned toward Earth—that which transmutes lead into gold, poison into medicine, and death into life. The philosopher's stone is a term describing the culmination of the alchemical mysteries.

But we can also read another meaning in this enigmatic saying about the power being complete if it is turned toward Earth. Completion of the circle comes when the spiritual power is shared with others, with companions, with cells or small groups, and with communities that in turn encourage and support the spiritual journey at their center. The individual journey takes one away from the fallen collective, the system, into solitude, and from solitude, into companionship of the quest.

What does a restored or regenerated community centered in the companionship of the quest look like? The hallmark of the fallen community, the collectivist and mechanized system, is that the individual is as nothing, while the hallmark of the regenerated or pristine community is that the individual flourishes and flowers as and beyond apparent individuality. The former is the erasure of self, which is why communist systems seek to obliterate culture and the past, and the latter is the fullness and transcendence of the self.

The regenerated community is a shared culture centered in the spiritual path. While in a degenerated society, there is no shared spiritual path, a regenerated community emerges around its spiritual center, which is the alchemical process of illumination. The path is shared in the sense that people in the community all understand its centrality and support and encourage this path even if they are not engaged in it themselves.

Such a community turns toward Earth in the sense of creating a way of life attuned to natural cycles, with seasonal rituals and traditions that clearly recognize its larger genetic-ethnic tribal and spiritual ancestors. It celebrates the coming of the light, the sustaining of the light, the rebirth of the light, in the life-giving recurrent seasonal cycle recognized by the ancient Europeans in their traditional calendrical events marking spring, summer, autumn, and winter, the equinoxes and solstices, the lunar and solar stages, and the constellations.

And there is something else we should mention here. Archaic European traditions had sacred stones—megaliths of many kinds, dolmens, standing stones, stone circles, and passage cairns at the top of hills or mountains. These are found still all across Britain, Wales, Scotland, Ireland, France, and indeed all of Europe into Central and even East Asia. Why sacred *stones*? Might there be a connection to the philosopher's stone, to the grailstone?

The alchemical process of light is related to the archaic traditions of Europe, representing the power turned toward Earth. This means divine, restorative power realized here on Earth, with others, harmonizing nature and the natural world with the human world through spiritual practice and ritual engagement. The alchemical vision is not only about us as individuals, or about self-development. It is about restoration of our primordial way of being, realizing together our original spiritual purity in nature, manifested in light and in the patterns of light, marked by stone, manifested in and through stone.

COMMUNITIES OF STONE AND LIGHT

The alchemical journey begins with our own development and awakening, but it does not end there. Like the grail quest, it is an individual quest that is also about the community of the whole. There is a wounded king who suffers; society is fallen and in disarray; and the grail quest is about that larger restoration or renewal. It turns out to be not so much about me as it is about us. Realizing this is also turning the power toward Earth.

Ultimately, the alchemical process of working with light is not only individual; it does not take place in one's own mind alone. Nor does it only involve a small group. The process is within us, but also beyond us as individuals. It is intimately personal, but it is also cosmological—that is, it engages the fundamental principles inherent in the cosmos. Regeneration, the restoration of the primordial, archaic state of purity, transmutes our fallen nature and also the fallen nature of the cosmos.

This was well understood by the ancients. Archaic Europe's sacred places, standing stones, cairns, and dolmens each have their specific light alignments, marking the movement of the Sun, the Moon, or specific constellations and stars. The stones in all their configurations mark the intersections of space and time by light. This light is eternal and temporal at once, both in time and beyond time, symbolized in the instantaneous bolt of lightning from above to below, in vertical standing stones, and later in stone columns.

The archaic European culture of stone and light was shared, first by the local community near the stones, second by those in the region, and third by the underlying broader culture across Europe and into Asia that is still visible wherever the stones are still standing. What was the purpose of this underlying archaic culture? To turn the power toward Earth, to align human, natural, and celestial with one another so that the human and natural worlds flourished.

Whenever you enter an area with megaliths, including cairns, you will often hear the folklore that says to take from the area of the stones or to damage the stones will bring about misfortune, bring upon you what we could call the curse of the stones. There is often a lingering fear of the archaic standing stones, a sense that they are a little otherworldly, numinous, and this protected them over the millennia. It also signals that there is more to the stones' presence than meets the eye.

What do the grailstone, the philosopher's stone, and the megaliths have in common? The power to transmute, to regenerate. While it may take a long time to find the grailstone or the philosopher's stone or the stone circle, their power of transmutation is itself immediate, like a lightning bolt flashing from sky to Earth. A fallen world and darkness and then—light!

Revelation of the archaic original and pure state, revelation of paradise, this is the hidden meaning of the sentinel stones like those that still keep watch over Britain, Wales, Scotland, and Ireland and that still work their magic. They stand guard now as they have for millennia, integrating the moving patterns of cosmic light in nature with the human world, their silent watch reminding us that a balanced, spiritual way of being beckons not only us as individuals, but us as nascent community, as living culture.

SHARED TRANSFORMATION

Alchemical lightwork is not only about us as individuals. It is about archaic knowledge and about what is greater than ourselves, beyond us. It is also about harmony between the human, natural, and spiritual realms—and about this Earth in relation to paradisal Earth. There is a very archaic Central Asian tradition in which, when someone died, a shaman would with a bird wing waft the deceased's soul into a stone, where it would remain until the deceased could be guided through a perilous passage to paradisal Earth, the Earth of celestial light.

Put another way, turning power toward Earth reveals power beyond Earth. Although we think that the otherworld and this physical world are completely distinct, that isn't really true. It's an illusion. As William

Law* and Jacob Böhme made clear, after death the soul doesn't "go" anywhere. Rather, its nature is revealed and experienced in whatever stage it finds itself. The otherworld is present now, but we aren't able to see it as it actually is.

Turning power toward Earth isn't necessarily something we do as an individual, but rather is a description of how, in the right conditions, flourishing is possible because inherent spiritual reality can manifest as it actually is. We forget that nature *wants* to flourish. People *want* to flourish. They yearn to do so. Turning power toward Earth means creating the conditions not only for us as individuals to flourish but for nature and community to do so as well.

One purpose of the standing stones and other megaliths, author John Michell told me, was to cast a spell of protection and prosperity over a region, to mark with light the hidden pathways and dimensions of the spiritual landscape so that the folk could flourish. This is also thought to be the purpose behind the ancient legendary island of Atlantis and of the mythical island kingdoms off the coast. Of course, Atlantis degenerated and collapsed, and perhaps things are not ideal in every way in the few remaining redoubts on Earth. Even in the kingdom of Bhutan, like anywhere else, people have conflicts, are fooled or are foolish, seek power, or are subject to whatever other human foibles any of us might be prey to or could imagine. And yet . . . they prove a different way of life is possible.

We do not have to live in a disenchanted, desolate world as atomized, nihilistic, cultureless individuals. We can engage in a quest. We can become better people. We can begin to explore and understand the mysteries of being human in a natural world full of mysteries. We can engage in the great adventure of our spiritual journey.

---

*William Law (1686–1761) was a contemplative in the tradition of Jacob Böhme. In addition to his books on topics like living a holy life, prayer, or Christian regeneration, Law provided an extraordinary translated version of Böhme's *Dialogues on the Supersensual Life* that we provide with commentary in our course called The Short Way: A Christian Mystical Path at the Hieros Institute. In the Law translation, the spiritual master directly discusses spiritual illumination and the nature of death and the afterlife in relation to spiritual illumination.

What's more, we can do so with others. This is part of the meaning of power being turned toward Earth—the power of our spiritual aspirations is turned toward our companions on the path who share our aspirations, and with whom, as with the companions on the quest for the Holy Grail, we seek not only the grailstone and illumination but also to restore the kingdom as a whole.

Even in an age of troubles, an age of degeneration and collapse, perhaps most of all then, envisioning a golden age is possible. And by envisioning it, we are creating its seeds, we are bringing it into being. The heart of a living culture is that it shelters and encourages a spiritual path for those in it. It surrounds, manifests, and supports those on the spiritual path of transformation.

Alchemy provides a way of understanding this path, both for an individual and for a community. Alchemy provides a way of understanding our movement from dark to light, the process that is our illumination. Of course, we make mistakes, we are human, we have our foibles and discontents—who would think otherwise? We begin in the nigredo, but we do not have to stay in the darkness. Moving through the stages of the alchemical transmutative process is possible. We can move toward the light and toward radiating light.

The *Emerald Tablet* tells us that its power is complete when it is turned toward Earth, when it is grounded, when the circle of spirit, nature, and humanity is joined, not separate from matter but illuminating it from within. Matter, again, is the house of light. When we become translucent, that which is around us also becomes translucent. We share the transformative light with others and with nature. That is what is meant by its power is complete.

We turn now in more detail to the stages of that process for individuals, couples, and community.

7
The Transmutative Process

Separating the earth from the fire, the subtle from the gross, with care and ingenuity.

EMERALD TABLET

From one perspective, we are fallen beings in a fallen world, meaning that as Buddhism recognizes, our lives are characterized by suffering. Sometimes the suffering is harshly painful, and sometimes it is subtle, but by and large we don't see ourselves in a paradisal world and indeed, during times of war, poverty, hunger, and so forth, we may experience it as nightmarish. But our fallenness is not just a matter of external circumstances. It is fundamentally inner as well as outer. How do we overcome this condition? Through the alchemical process of healing, restoration, and illumination.

The alchemical process has at its center the understanding that primordial man was originally in a balanced, pure, paradisiacal state of innocence. In this understanding, summarized by Dionysius Andreas Freher,* primordial humanity's "heavenly Mercury" manifested a clear

---

*Dionysius Andreas Freher (1649–1728) was an accomplished practitioner in the tradition of Jacob Böhme. He was a mystic and alchemist who published illuminating illustrations and commentary on the spiritual-alchemical transformative path. An important introduction to his work was published by Charles Musès, titled *Illumination on Jacob Boehme: The Work of Dionysius Andreas Freher*.

fire, nourished by pure spiritual oil, and gave forth a glorious, bright light. But when the pure elements of primordial humanity became imbalanced and mixed, fallen Mercury gave way to anguish, and humanity was divided in itself and against itself. Alchemy provides a way of understanding both this fall and the return to an original, pure, unfallen state. Through alchemy, the divided two again become one.

Fundamental to understanding this alchemical process of restoration are the planets, understood not only as physical objects in orbit around the Sun but also as richly evocative mythic symbols alive both in the cosmos and in us. We alluded earlier to the roles of the lightbearers—the Sun, the Moon, and the constellations—in relation to megalithic Europe and now delve into the symbolic roles of the planets in the alchemical process of regeneration.

LIGHT QUALITIES AND CHARACTERISTICS OF THE PLANETS

The planets here can be seen as qualities or kinds of light. The Sun's light has a very different quality from that of the Moon—the Sun is harshly bright; the Moon's is a more gentle white. Mars the warrior is reddish, and each of the other planets has its own distinctive mythic symbolism and hue. Astrology, like alchemy, has very archaic roots and cannot be understood without realizing that essentially astrology incorporates mathematical temporospatial calculations with ancient mythic light symbols into a comprehensive, integrated, psychospiritual multidimensional system. Hence astrology in India is known as Jyotish, the science of light.

The nature of a planet's light in this tradition depends on whether it is fallen or in its pure state. Its nature is expressed in psychospiritual terms. Psychologically, our fallen condition is characterized by fallen Mercury (intelligence) being subjected to Saturn (constriction) and Mars (wrath), and out of their fallen synergy emerges our false sense of self, or selfishness. Our restored condition comes about through the transmutation of these dark, fiery, restrictive qualities by love and light.

Mercury, Saturn, and Mars in their fallen state are the dark triad of rationality subsumed to restrictive self-referentiality and wrath. This is our familiar condition, being caught up in reactivity, anxiety about what others think, fear, jealousy, anger, and greed that color what we see and how we react. In alchemy, this is the black, the nigredo. How do we get beyond it into the white, the albedo/candeo?

The answer among the planets is through the Sun, Venus, and Jupiter. The Sun is illumination, breaking forth into the dark triad, which of course resists mightily. And Venus is love, the lovingness that gives herself up into the fallen properties and transforms them, softening their wrathfulness with the help of Jupiter's generosity. The illumination of the Sun and the permeation of the dark triad with love produces first the white-yellow stage (*citrinitas*) and then finally the red (*rubedo*).

The white stage is that of the initial purification—it is illumination in the darkness, and so is closely linked to the yellow stage, the stage in which the inner Sun radiates out from the heart and illuminates the various wheels or centers in the body. The alchemical process as a whole in this tradition is the invocation of the light, and the white-yellow stage is the light overcoming the darkness. The Sun, Venus, and Jupiter represent aspects of this illuminative process.

This transformative process reunites the planets into an integrated, balanced whole, restoring them to their original qualities. In their fallen aspects, the planets represent the disarray of the soul, its capture by negative emotions or characteristics, but in their original pristine aspects, the planets work together in harmony to transmute the world into paradise and us into our original paradisal nature. Jupiter and Venus are the benefic king and queen, generous and loving, in the radiance of the Sun.

You will notice that the planets are male or female in nature. The male planets are Sol (the Sun), Jupiter, Mars, Saturn, and Mercury; the female are Luna (the Moon) and Venus. Ultimately, the two tinctures, the male and female, must be united into one, and this is the androgyne, or "youth-maiden," the shining resurrected or regenerated being that includes both male and female qualities in harmony. You can see this image in some alchemical sequences like the magnificent *Splendor Solis*, *Rosarium Philosophorum*, or *Aurora Consurgens*.

But what is the transmutative power that brings about this process? As Dionysius Freher remarks, the dark triad cannot be transmuted from itself or on its own accord—required is power from beyond the fallen nature of the being that accomplishes this process of restoration so that the primordial planetary qualities can be expressed. In Christianity, this transmutative power is Christ, metaphysical or transcendent light. The Hermetic tradition refers to Hermes Trismegistus, to whom the *Emerald Tablet* is attributed.

THE PROCESS OF TRANSMUTATION

The *Emerald Tablet* refers to the transmutative process as separating "the earth from the fire, the subtle from the gross, with care and ingenuity." In us, this means allowing the alchemical process to work, so that we are no longer as caught up in outward distractions and reactions, in anger and fear, jealousy and aversion. We are no longer as caught up in wanting this or seeking to avoid that. We separate the subtle from the gross. Our emotional reactivity becomes less coarse and wild; we are no longer under the sway of the unregenerated planets, to use the alchemical language.

This process entails water and fire because water purifies and fire transmutes. It separates the dross from the pure, the gross from the subtle. Purification and transmutation are difficult as we confront and deal with our shit, in colloquial terms. The light and love are here too, of course, just as there is light in fire, but later the light and love are clearer and calmer, pellucid.

This transmutative process does not happen just once, or instantly. Hence the *Emerald Tablet* refers to working with "care and ingenuity" over time. The alchemical process we are discussing here is measured in years, in the gradual transmutation of our life. How we relate to the natural world, how we relate to other people, how we relate to the spiritual realm . . . all of these become more gentle, more insightful, more free. Working with "care and ingenuity" means that we are confronted with dilemmas and challenges in the course of life, and the alchemical process means illuminating these, so the divine light transmutes and blesses them.

The transmutative power in the light is loving-kindness, which expresses itself in different ways depending on the context. The feminine planetary energies, and especially Venus, represent this transmutative power of love. But in this alchemical process, Venus is not met with a warm embrace by the dark triad of emotional reactivity. Instead, the dark triad of reactivity, Saturn, Mars, and Mercury, respectively restriction and fear, anger, and selfish discursive rationality, seek to overcome and ruin Venus and her loving-kindness. But her transmutative energy eventually combines with their higher aspects (discipline, right action, and consciousness) in the process of regeneration.

In this alchemical tradition, love is how light expresses itself. It isn't that light is somehow separate from love, but rather that to the extent we are caught up in our own reactivity and confusion, we are separate from both of them at once. And the alchemical process of transmutation is that gradually light and love become clearer for us. Working with light is first of all working with our own darkness and allowing it to be illuminated. Only then can the light illuminate and help others.

So the alchemical process can be understood in natural terms of invoking and realizing the light, and in our world, the strongest light is the Sun's. Hence Plotinus, the great Platonic gnostic of antiquity, referred to the experience of seeing the inner light as the Sun rising, illuminating the mind and chasing away all shadows. This revelation of light can be invoked by being in the Sun's light and envisioning its radiance dawning within our heart. Paying homage to the Sun, invoking the Sun. And this inward Sun's light can radiate in darkness, for as was said of the ancient Mysteries by the ancient Roman author

Apuleius in his novel *The Golden Ass*, at the culmination of the initiation, he tells us directly, the Sun dawned at midnight.

We can invoke the regenerate, pure qualities of the other planets as well, all of which in their primordial nature, in harmony, are beneficent and embody different virtues. Jupiter is generosity, Saturn order, Venus loving-kindness, Mercury clear communication, Mars courage, the Moon gentleness, and the Sun regalness. The alchemical process means becoming a better human being and realizing our original purity, which is also the primordial illuminated and harmonious purity of the cosmos.

An essential part of the alchemical process is invoking the golden chain of those who have themselves accomplished the Great Work, including the revealer or primordial figure of the tradition. In the Hermetic tradition, this is Hermes, and in Vajrayana Buddhism, it is Padmasambhava, also known as Guru Rinpoche. In the Christian tradition, it is Christ who underwent death and resurrection, thus opening the way for us to also be reborn and enter into paradise.

But even if we choose not to be formally affiliated with or draw upon a particular religious tradition, we can engage in this alchemical process of illumination because it is natural, and it reflects timeless principles in us as human beings and in the cosmos. It also provides a template for restoring or creating genuine, profoundly ecologically balanced, enduring communities, a template for the future and, as we will see, for future cultures.

While we moderns often want to believe that we are entirely self-sufficient and don't need archaic traditions, the truth is that we wouldn't even have the concepts of alchemy, let alone the symbolic maps for the process, without the ancients having provided them to us. Alchemy exists as a way of understanding because they gave it to us.

Our elders conveyed the alchemical process elliptically, through ciphers, through enigmatic images and aphorisms, because it cannot be reduced to inputs and outputs, like machinery or chemistry. It brings together different worlds, and what it alludes to is not limited only to the material but also integrates the physical, psychic, and spiritual. The planets are physical bodies, but in the traditional understanding, they are also psychological and spiritual; they are outside us, in space, but they are also qualities within us.

TRANSFORMATION THROUGH MALE-FEMALE UNION

The alchemical process, because it is integrative, does not exist only in us as discrete individuals. Of course, it requires us as individuals to be engaged in it, but it is also cosmological and metaphysical, working with nature in order to effect the transmutation. It is not complete reintegration if it involves only individuation.

The alchemical process can be intensified through relationship, if both parties are consciously engaged in the process. Of course, the process is intensified because an intimate relationship can bring up and manifest our deepest challenges and issues. Essentially, it raises the stakes quite a bit both ways: it can accelerate your progress, or it can devolve into profound challenges. But being in a relationship dedicated to mutual transformation is very powerful and is symbolized in the figures of the king and the queen in alchemical illustrations like those in the *Rosarium Philosophorum*, the famous and beautiful set of alchemical images.

In the *Rosarium* images, you see the alchemical process expressed in the progressive union of a male and a female figure that transform through the sequence of images into a divine couple that becomes an androgyne, or youth-maiden. This process of transformation can be likened in some respects to what we find in tantric traditions. Male-female union expresses and accelerates spiritual illumination understood as the transcendent union but also transcendence of male and female, as the two become one.

The images in the color insert are from a version of the *Rosarium Philosophorum*, now housed at the University of Glasgow. They show some of the stages of alchemical transmutation in the form of a uniting king and queen, first clothed, then nude, then uniting into a single androgyne being with two heads. In the sequence, you can see how the changes undergone by the king and the queen also involve the Sun and Moon. In the penultimate image shown here, we see the resplendent winged solar unity, what is called the *Splendor Solis* in another famous set of images.

The union of the Sun and Moon in the couple result from the transmutation process undergone by the king and the queen, and this process—because it involves a king and queen—can also be understood as having implications beyond two individuals. It is an individual process, in that the king and queen can be understood to be within an individual, but it also can be seen as a process involving a man and a woman. And beyond the couple, the process has implications for natural and human community: it is a restoration that transcends individuals. Regeneration of the sacred couple is regeneration of nature, the family, and the community.

We see in this sequence of images the restoration of primordial nature through the primordial couple. Fallen nature, human beings divided against one another and against nature, give way in this process to unification and restoration of androgynous, united, and balanced humanity and nature. The couple is key to the process, of course. And the result is the restoration of our original angelic nature, symbolized by the solar-angelic head with wings illuminating the plinth below. Nature is transformed and restored to its unfallen, primordial condition.

Family can also be understood in terms of the alchemical process. A couple's relationship is the center and ground of the family, of course. But our family, including the family into which we were born, is also a kind of mirror and means for understanding who we are and who we can be, expressed and addressed in terms of virtues, such as patience, generosity, kindness, and clarity.

Imagine what it would be like to be part of a family that broadly understands and is engaged in an alchemical understanding of life and in transmutation and awakening. In the Himalayas, this is what one has, broadly speaking, in Tibetan Buddhism, where everyone in a family has a Buddhist understanding even if some are more devoted than others. There is a shared, collective orientation toward spiritual progress.

Now imagine what it would be like to be part of a community that in turn supports the family in this alchemical understanding. The individual is supported by the family, which in turn is supported by the community, in shared transformation. There is an alchemical cultural continuity, which we see in the Tibetan Buddhist tradition prior to the Chinese invasion and occupation, and even after, especially in diaspora. And of course, the Buddhist tradition has expressed itself in alchemical terms, as we saw in Nagarjuna the alchemist. Alchemy is very congenial to Buddhism. And we do find much that is analogous to Buddhism in the Western alchemical tradition.

Perhaps you have seen the magnificent images of the *Splendor Solis* series. You will notice, if you study the series, that its images involve a transmuted landscape and community, including folk, animals, earth, water, and sky. Are such images only alluding to a transmuted individual? Or are they alluding instead to a greater process, one that integrates a realm or region? There are still more mysteries here than first meet the eye.

First is the individual's drive to seek the path of individual flowering. Without this, there is no alchemical path. Then there is the alchemical couple, male and female, king and queen, who together assist one another in fully realizing the alchemical path. And there is the alchemical group of comrades, who together experience the alchemy of spiritual friends, or coexplorers. And there are those in the community or region that join with them, or who begin to recognize their hidden effects.

What the *Emerald Tablet* refers to as the separation of the subtle from the gross is the continuing process of purification. The spiritual process is not linear. It occurs more like a spiral, where we return to the same point again but from a different and deeper perspective. Purification, overcoming our shadows or our darknesses, happens through the power of the light but also through our continuing aspiration to become pellucid. This aspiration goes beyond us as individuals, and as we share it with another, and with others, it transmutes us and our world.

This is a primordial spiritual community. It has existed in the most remote past; it exists now; and it will exist in the future, on the other side of the collapse of technological modernity. It will always exist. Although the alchemical transmutative process is found in different religious traditions, it is fundamentally a human process that draws on elements of nature both within and beyond us, and it is perennial—that is, perpetually there to be rediscovered.

PART THREE
The Yellow

8
The Mysteries Reborn

Ascend wisely from the earth to heaven, and then again descend to earth, uniting what is above and below. Thus you will realize the glory of the whole world, and all obscurity and darkness will fly far away from you.

EMERALD TABLET

The yellow stage in alchemy (citrinitas) is the golden or solar light that penetrates us and all that is around us. White is the stage of purification, and with the yellow, we fully enter the phase of solar tincturing that goes beyond us as individuals. Here, we will explore the ancient Mysteries, the collective experience of illumination in which the sun was said to shine at midnight, meaning that the golden light illuminated all, and penetrated through the darkness, transfiguring us and all that surrounds us. Could the Mysteries be reborn in us, in a new era?

Of course, from a historical perspective, the ancient Mystery traditions belonged to antiquity, and since they were discontinued in the period of late antiquity, one certainly can't speak of the Mysteries being reborn. In fact, we don't even know for sure how the Mysteries in antiquity were celebrated because initiates were sworn to secrecy and, to a remarkable degree, honored their promise. And so we are left with a set of tantalizing clues, all of which, relating to the Mysteries at Samothrace, I discussed in

Entering the Mysteries. Here, though, we are going to explore a different territory, one that belongs not to the past but to the future, in what we can call a thought experiment. For while it's true that the Mysteries are gone in one sense, in another they may be still very much with us.

What were the ancient Mysteries? We alluded to them earlier, and here will not go into them in detail, but it may be helpful give a brief overview. The ancient Mysteries were devoted to different gods and goddesses and had specific centers where their rites were celebrated. The Mystery center at Eleusis and the Mystery complex on the island of Samothrace are the most well known from the Greco-Roman world, but there were many Mystery cults in antiquity, and they varied widely, from the mother-goddess cults, known collectively as Magna Mater (the Great Mother), to the goddess Isis and the horseman-god cults, each manifesting a different ancient origin and tradition.

THE MYSTERIES AS SHARED ILLUMINATION

The Mysteries at the island of Samothrace had at their center primordial man, an integrated being of light, represented and guarded by a male figure with an erection (vitality), and were commemorated by an initiatic ring of iron, symbolizing the magnetic power of the initiation. The purpose of the initiation was to experience this reintegration and illumination, which means to die before mortal death and so to know what happens after death, assuring a good afterlife.

As we go farther back, we find the enigmatic Orphic Mysteries, of which a considerable record exists, not only in the remarks of ancient Greek or Roman authors but also in a body of Orphic literature, including many tablets of gold on which were inscribed Orphic texts. The Orphic Mysteries hearken back to Thrace, the wild forested region north of Greece that includes what is now known as Bulgaria.

Orphism, as a main conduit of secret knowledge from archaic Europe into the Greek world, is truly mysterious. It has special meaning to us because, while belonging to archaic Europe before the emergence of Greece and then Rome, it also can be understood as a model for the future. Orphism, with its itinerant priest-initiators and initiates, is a decentralized spirituality emphasizing its direct lineages of initiates, much like Vajrayana Buddhism. It resembles the Ngakpa tradition in Nyingma Buddhism, a nonmonastic form of transmission with lay initiatic spiritual practitioners.

Orphism was a tradition of formulas, many of which we know because they were inscribed on gold tablets. The most famous such formula has many variants, but it includes the following phrase: "I am the child of Earth and starry Heaven."

One such gold tablet reads as follows:

I am dry with thirst and I perish.
But let me drink from the ever-flowing spring on the right,
by the cypress.
"Who are you? Where are you from?"
I am the son of Earth and starry Heaven.

What does this mean? It is a formula for the deceased, who in the formula is given clear directions (turn right, to the water by the cypress tree). Then the deceased will be challenged, and the password answer is "I am the son of Earth and starry Heaven."

Some tablets refer clearly to the initiate becoming deified or godlike after death, leaving the light of the Sun and entering a new light, being presented with challenges (turning left is warned against), and then directly confronted by guardians to whom one must answer, "I am the child of Earth and Heaven, but my race is of Heaven." Then one may drink of the refreshing water and take one's place as a hero or initiate (sometimes noted as an initiate of chthonic Persephone), who can enjoy the paradisal meadow and groves of the afterlife. Philosophically, this could be expressed this way: having come from the One, we return to the One.

Orphism represents an archaic tradition with at least one analogue, visible in ancient pre-Buddhist Tibetan tradition. The mapping of afterlife states and a tradition of guiding the newly dead exists in contemporary Tibetan Buddhism in *Bardo Thodrol*, or *Tibetan Book of the Dead*, of course, and what we find in Orphism is actually quite analogous: oral and textual lineages of an archaic religion of light, guiding the deceased through the dangers of the afterlife to paradise. This suggests that there was a truly an archaic tradition that Orphism continues, as does Vajrayana Buddhism.

Here we are looking at inscribed gold tablets of a Mystery religion whose origins go back before the historical record, in turn contributing to the flowering of the larger, more centralized Mystery centers, to Greek culture, including the great Platonic school of philosophers and theurges, that is, the practitioners of light at the headwaters of Western culture. A vital part of this transmission is a set of mysterious texts known as the *Chaldean Oracles*.

In these enigmatic texts, we are given instructions on how to practice a religion of light. We are told, for instance, to array ourselves from head to toe with a brilliant light, to be armed in mind and soul with a triple-barbed strength and concentration. In this tradition, which I discuss in detail in *Religion of Light*, we are instructed to purify our luminous body, the "delicate vehicle of the soul," "to perceive the shape of light which has been stretched forth." In short, we need to turn our attention away from the "light-hating world" and toward illumination.

THE MYSTERIES OF LIGHT

What happened to these mysteries of light? What we see historically is that the ancient Mysteries take on different forms. The Egyptian Mysteries later are transmitted in a new form to the Greek world; the ancient Mysteries of the Great Mother also feed into new forms of Mysteries of the goddess; the ancient cult at Samothrace takes on later forms even into the Roman era; and the Christian Mysteries continue the earlier mysteries of light.

Of course, most people in the Protestant, Catholic, and Orthodox worlds do not consciously think of Christianity as a Mystery tradition, even though in reality the Catholic and Orthodox traditions do refer to the Mysteries of Christianity, including among these baptism, the Eucharist, marriage, and death (unction). Still, when you reflect on it, you can see that Christ is the Logos, the divine Sun, the bringer of light—even into the darkness of hell itself (the harrowing of hell). And from this perspective, as Protestant mystic Jacob Böhme and his successors made clear, Christianity is a Mystery religion.

This is important to understand because, as Dionysius Freher observed, he who is trapped does not have the means to escape the trap on his own, but has to rely on another, the "workmaster" or "workman" who has the means to rescue him. In essence, this is the meaning of the mysteries of light: we who are trapped in our own selfhood cannot escape our selfhood via our own self or on our own; we reach toward the light as the light is reaching toward us. Freher remarks that we do not accomplish and cannot accomplish the alchemical process on our own but rather must rely on the divine—the light—to accomplish it in us.

I am mentioning this vital point here because in the age of materialism and "self-help," it became common for people to believe, "*I can do it on my own. I don't need guides or gurus, or revealed religion. I'm sufficient to transform myself,*" which is the literal meaning, after all, of *self-help*. But Freher is right. Can *I*, on my own, save myself? The question answers itself. The self, by seeking to resolve the suffering caused by the self, very easily ends up generating more or less subtle ways of reinforcing the self.

With all this as background, then, we are broaching here the question of how the archaic Mysteries could recur in new forms, as part of the larger role of the alchemical process not just for the individual but also for a community, communities, and culture. Of course, an individual and a couple or a small group can engage in the alchemical process.

This can happen in any social circumstance, even under a tyrannical, authoritarian, antireligious state. Archaic spiritual culture can recur regardless of a seemingly dominant anti-culture.

The alchemical process we are discussing, which clearly has a Western cultural history, nonetheless is ultimately a human process that reflects truth prior to its cultural expression, beyond and yet embedded in particular religious and cultural expression. Hermetism and Platonism recur in different religious contexts and times, as both are pointing to fundamental truths that we as human beings can also perceive and experience for ourselves. The *Emerald Tablet* puts it this way: if you ascend to heaven and descend to earth, uniting the two, all darkness will fly from you. Objectively, it is saying, if you make the two into one, this is what will happen: the darkness will disappear. This process manifests in different traditions, but it is ultimately about a process inherently available to us as human beings.

CAN THE MYSTERIES BE REBORN?

By now we have seen clearly that there is a long Western tradition of light, of illumination, of what can be termed lightwork that took many forms. The Mysteries in archaic Europe themselves took different forms, yet shared their emphasis on illumination and its connection to paradise after death. Christianity itself can be understood as a continuation of this current for those that recognize it. But all of this raises questions about possible future forms.

Is a rebirth of the Mysteries possible? Under what conditions? How? Our answer to such questions depends upon our perspective. For a materialist caught in time, a dogmatic believer in historism, of course no such rebirth is possible, probably not even those of the past that already happened. Such an individual will claim each manifestation has no relationship to the others, was a result of economic or social forces, that sort of thing, and if something were to emerge in the future, it too would be like this, discrete, a result of dialectical materialism, or whatever.

It's true that forms of expression and manifestation vary. Not all the Mysteries were the same. But it is possible that in the Mysteries, as in the alchemical process, the spiritual is objectively valid in its own right, that what is timeless and belongs to the timeless can manifest in any time *because* it is beyond time. Of course, we can dismiss the Mysteries or alchemical process as fictional or delusional, but since they both manifested in multiple times and places, in what I have termed an ahistorical continuity, perhaps what is there cannot be dismissed with the wave of a hand. There were alchemists in antiquity; there were medieval alchemists; there were Renaissance alchemists; there are alchemists today; there will be alchemists in the future.

But with the Mysteries, you have something still more puzzling: From where did they come? There was undoubtedly a revealer, a figure or group at the tradition's headwaters through whom the revelation and the practices came. The supernatural entered the natural through them and with them. The light was strong enough in them that they could, to some degree, share it, and that sharing began the tradition.

Authentic Mysteries have supernatural, transcendent origins and cannot be artificially constructed or compelled; they come from beyond us. So how and when a Mystery tradition could appear, who could say? Perhaps only when there are people who could receive and transmit them; perhaps only in the early phase of a nascent culture; perhaps only when some people have prepared themselves for them. What is timeless is always nascent. What is true is always true, and therefore ready to be born anew.

Let us look not only back into the archaic, but ahead into the new or future archaic. What is on the other side of the dissolution of our age, the fall of materialism and technologism, the collapse of communist or other regimes? Only barbarism? Or is it possible to look ahead and scry the development of new cultures, a rebirth of the archaic in a new and renewed age? In the ancient way of speaking, the Iron Age, or Kali Yuga, is not the end of time or of the world, for after it comes, in the great cycle, a new golden age.

For there is an alchemy of individuals, an alchemy of couples, an alchemy of groups, and an alchemy of cultures. Are we doomed to live in an age of perpetual decline, coarsening, and cultural destruction, or can we look up over the horizon and begin to see the outlines of emerging new cultures and new ways of being in the world in which we can naturally manifest our higher, alchemical purpose of realizing who and where we truly are?

The Mysteries have to do with the alchemy of cultures. They are about the revelation and transmission of salvific light in the darkness. They are about the mystery of what seeks to reveal the light, what seeks to help us transform and become better people, to create a shared ethos and spiritual understanding at the heart of a new culture, paradoxically, in a specific place, a specific landscape, a specific people and time. Alchemical lightwork is making such a rebirth possible; it is envisioning and making way for it.

This is what is meant by the *Emerald Tablet* when it tells us to "ascend wisely from the earth to heaven, and then again descend to earth, uniting what is above and below." When we do, we will "realize the glory of the whole world, and all obscurity and darkness will fly far away from [us]." This union is transcendence in and beyond immanence—it is beyond and illuminates the light of nature. A renewed way of life is calling from beyond us as individuals.

9
Light Eternal

This is the power of all powers, as it overcomes all that is subtle, and permeates everything solid.

EMERALD TABLET

Light bursting forth in darkness is instantaneous. Out of nothing—light. From a seemingly endless darkness, the absence of light, and then, when there is a source of illumination—light, and with light, sight. This is a mystery silently celebrated by ancient standing stones aligned with the rising of the solstice Sun or in a stone cairn that is dark nearly all year, but on one day, the Sun's beam illuminates the cavern so some petroglyphs are suddenly visible.

Do we create the light? Or is the light simply there when the conditions are right? We can arrange the conditions, of course. But the light itself is not ours; we don't own it or make it; we arrange the conditions in which it appears, making a fire, lighting a candle or lamp, turning on an electrical light. When the conditions are present, there is light.

Alchemy can be understood as creating those conditions. It has at its center the recognition that humanity and nature were originally pure and unfallen and that although we appear to be in a fallen state now, it is possible to restore primordial purity to ourselves and to nature. Alchemy is the process of this restoration. Nature is out of balance, but the balance can be restored. We humans are out of balance, disharmonious, but our balance can be restored too. And these two are linked.

RIDING THE TIGER

At some point you may come across the phrase "ride the tiger" or "ride the lion" as counsel for how to navigate in a fallen world. But what does this phrase actually mean? One author said that it originated in an anecdote about a yogi who, to avoid being eaten by a tiger, leapt upon its back and rode it to exhaustion, and the author claimed that people in a fallen, debased society are like that yogi and have to ride the tiger, that is, harness the fallen society to do their will.

A Greek Orthodox friend refers to "riding with the lion," and here is a very different understanding. There are several saints associated with lions, but my friend is referring to the legend of St. Mamas, the protector of animals, who had a docile lion as a companion that some said even allowed St. Mamas to ride it into town. Of course, the lion could be understood as the divine companion, or as a symbol of Christ's regal power, riding *with* not *on* the lion. The underlying idea is alchemical—that nature can be restored to its original, primordial harmony.

Then there is the Tiger's Nest in the remote mountainous country of Bhutan. This famous monastery is perched impossibly high on the side of a mountain crag, and although you might have seen it, it's probable that no one mentioned how the Tiger's Nest got there. The answer, according to legend, is that Guru Rinpoche, the great founding guru of Tibetan Buddhism, came to Bhutan flying with a tigress. And the tigress, it is said, was in heat or, some say, pregnant and volatile, unpredictable. The tigress and Guru Rinpoche could fly up to and light together on the high crag, and what is more, where they landed, an entire monastery appeared magically. This is the legend. Of course, the monastery is quite real, though its construction through ordinary means seems virtually impossible. Hence the legend.

And this legend represents a very different understanding than the idea of riding a tiger to wear it down. It is, rather, a legend expressing something like *fiat lux*, or "let there be light." Guru Rinpoche and the tigress together were somehow magically able to manifest an outward sign of the harmonious unity of man, nature, and transcendence in the spontaneous creation of a building impossibly perched on a crag high above a valley vista.

Can you see the differences between these three instances? The notion of a yogi manhandling a tiger is not quite the same as a saint who befriends a lion, and neither of these is the same as the magical unity of the spiritual master flying with a volatile tigress. This last one is mysterious, magical, and totally outside the bounds of convention, so much so that we really don't even quite know what to think of it.

Here we might return to the ancient alchemist, Zosimos of Panopolis, who wrote that all the transformations of nature, and of nature and spirit, are "One Thing," "of One Nature, acting upon itself." Nature is "of one kind but many colors," regulated by lunar and solar rhythms and times, through which the "One Nature" self-transforms. All nature emerges out of and returns to itself; it's one nature, acting upon itself.

THE POWER OF ALL POWERS

The *Emerald Tablet* refers to the "power of all powers" that "overcomes all that is subtle and permeates everything solid." To what is it referring? All such twilight language is enigmatic, eluding the kind of rationalistic conceptual pinning down to which we are so accustomed in a materialistic worldview. There, everything is potentially, perhaps even actually explained, or ex-plained, that is, flattened out, whereas alchemical language goes in the opposite direction, toward allusion and ellipsis.

We find ourselves in the Iron Age, or the Kali Yuga, a fallen age in which society, for all its technical achievements, is fragmented, atomized, mercantile, debased, anticultural, iconoclastic, celebrating that which should be shameful, while treating as shameful that which should be celebrated. An antispiritual and anticultural age. In such an era, what is possible?

This is a point from which the alchemical path can guide us. The first stage, as we have seen, is the dissolution, the black, the tearing down, and the losing of illusions. We have been taught lies, we have lived lies, but now those are falling away and in the darkness we find ourselves searching, seeking light. When the light dawns, we have reached the white stage. But the white is not the end of the path. Within the white dawns the golden Sun, the yellow phase of the citrinitas, permeated more fully by the divine light, but this is also not the final stage.

As we will see in detail later, but must introduce now, there is another phase ahead, marked by the red, or rubedo, and the marriage of the king and queen, the red and the white. In this phase appears the philosopher's stone, and what is that? It is the means for the transmutation of nature, of ourselves and the world around us, and is thus the culmination of the Great Work. In some alchemical series, the very final phase is marked by an image of Christ, suggesting that Christ is the true philosopher's stone. The philosopher's stone culminates the alchemical work and transmutes both us and the world to their primordial, pure state.

Conventionally, and especially in a materialistic society, we think of everything as solid, moving through time in a measurable, predictable way. We live as discrete subjects in a world of manipulable objects. But what if that's not how things really are? What if there is a "power of powers" that permeates all things both subtle and solid? The One, or the One Nature, you could call it. Ultimately, alchemy is telling us there is a fundamentally different way of being.

In arithmosophy—the spiritual implications of numbers—there is the One, and then there is the many. All successive numbers exist within the One. Unity precedes multiplicity, which inheres within it. All gradations, all numerical multiplicity, small and large, is affirmed, not negated, by the unity out of which they emerge and in which they subsist.

Plotinus put this a different way. He tells us that at the center is pure, brilliant light, in a circle or sphere, and beyond this is another sphere, less brilliant, but still illuminating, and then a third sphere, which needs the light of another. The great light shines in the center, and the farther from the center one goes, the farther one is from the source of light. Far from the center, one is ensnared in corporeal nature—that is, in multiplicity and in one's reactions to it.

The light is the One. Light is consciousness, and consciousness inheres in multiplicity. It is only that we have become ensnared in our own reactions to multiplicity that we have forgotten the light. This light is inherent in all things; and the arithmosophic expression of this is that all numbers or multiplicity is inherent in the One.

Alchemical transmutation has at its center the understanding that even though the world and we are fallen beings, ultimately that fallenness is itself an illusion. For the transmutation to be possible, the original or primordial purity must still exist. If fallenness were existentially true, then that would mean that the One, or the light, had ceased in some ultimate sense. What alchemy tells us is that restoration or regeneration is possible because the Light is always present, even when we have forgotten it.

Because we are fallen beings, we must return to the light gradually, becoming more and more pellucid. And yet at the same time, the light remains instantaneously present. All of this is symbolically visible in the great alchemical treatises and accompanying sets of images, like *Rosarium Philosophorum*, originally a set of woodcuts in black and white and later in striking colors, as in the Ferguson manuscript housed in the University of Glasgow.

THE ALCHEMICAL PROCESS IN IMAGES

The first image in the Rosarium series is of the fountain of life, a perpetual fountain with three outlets pouring down into a basin—the virgin's milk, the vinegar spring, and the water of life—which combine in the basin to form the water of Mercury. This is the perpetual fountain of life, the source of the process, also termed the prima materia. The milk is female, the vinegar male, and these two principles combine with the water of life (aqua vitae). The whole process is forecast in this image.

In plate 2, we see the male and female principles as king and queen. They are fully dressed in royal garb, the king standing on the Sun, the queen on the Moon. They offer one another flowers, and above the flowers is a descending bird, symbolizing the spiritual power of the holy spirit descending into the crossed flowers whose stems point to the king's and queen's hearts. Plate 3 shows both of them nude, with inscriptions saying that Sol and Luna (Sun and Moon) become husband and wife.

Later illustrations in the sequence show the nude queen and king embracing, joining together in union, and becoming one in a nude androgyne figure with two heads (see plate 5). Some versions of the eleventh illustration show the nude, embracing, wingèd king and queen in water, with the queen's right hand grasping the king's erect phallus, while the king's left hand is touching the queen near her right nipple, suggesting the circulation of energies under the heading of "Fermentation."

The twelfth illustration in the Ferguson manuscript is "Illumination," (see plate 6) which, as we saw earlier, is of a single winged head with golden rays emerging from it, sitting atop a square pedestal within which appears to be golden fire. Around the head are clouds, indicating sky, so the image joins the Earth and the heavens, or heaven. The image of a winged head is, in early Christianity and later in theosophical Christianity, how angels are depicted—winged consciousness in flight, one could say.

This is, of course, not the entire sequence, as there are too many images, and there is too much in the series for us to fully discuss here. I draw attention to this sequence, though, because it illustrates the alchemical process and illumination in relation to man and woman, a primordial couple who join together and become a single angelic being that explicitly signifies illumination.

The Glasgow version of the *Rosarium* sequence concludes with a Christian image, the final one being the resurrected Christ standing above the opened grave, his head radiating the solar golden rays. This image corresponds very well to the esoteric Christian tradition we see in the writing of Jacob Böhme and Dionysius Freher, where the culmination of the alchemical process is achievement of the resurrection lightbody after death.

One way to understand this sequence is in light of the alchemical process as discussed by Dionysius Freher, which is akin to Eastern tantric traditions in a number of ways. These images in the *Rosarium* show the royal couple clothed, then disrobed, and progressively joining. Only part of this sequence is explicitly sexual: the image in some versions where the female figure is touching or holding the male figure's erect phallus, while he is touching her right breast. In this image, we see the circulation and sublimation of sexual energy serving the higher purpose of union, as we see also in Tantrism.

It is worth observing here that the alchemical tradition of Jacob Böhme refers to and shows chakras, often translated as "wheels," at central points in the spiritual body, notably in the area below the solar plexus, and at the solar plexus, the heart, the throat, the forehead, and the crown of the skull. In the spiritually regenerated and illuminated man, these are consolidated into the radiant heart. There are numerous chakra systems in Hinduism, with different chakra maps and associations, but even in the primary one known broadly in the West, and in Buddhism as well, there certainly are parallels with the Böhmean sequence.

Some academics feel moved to dismiss the obvious correspondences here between Eastern and Western traditions, and you might ask why. A major reason is that they continue, in a contemporary materialistic paradigm, a variant secular form of early exoteric Christian rejection of the esoteric path made available by Böhme and others, before and after him. Just as Böhme's own pastor sought to prevent Böhme from publishing his profound spiritual writings, so too do some contemporary materialistic academics seek to block those that take mysticism, including the alchemical process, seriously on its own terms as a path. They seek to extend into contemporary discourse the exoteric Christian rejection of inner process.

THE ALCHEMICAL PROCESS AND THE ETERNAL LIGHT

What does the alchemical process have to do with eternal light (lux aeterna)? As we have seen, the alchemical process in the *Rosarium* goes through stages, culminating in illumination and resurrection or regeneration. In the alchemical tradition, the primordial light is always there. Regeneration is always present. It's just that we don't see it. We with our dense materialistic and ideological robes, our confusion, have much to let go of before we can begin to glimpse the light.

Of course, there is the possibility that the veils fall away, and we can see clearly at once. This is riding *with* the tiger, or with the lion. But it is more likely that we need to engage in a process, so that the veils gradually thin and disappear, and we see more and more clearly. This is what Plotinus was describing at various times in his *Enneads*, where he said that being intimate with the higher world is the only love that can truly satisfy our inner longing, so that we become through this profound inner intimacy pure intellectual light itself, weightless, buoyant, full of spiritual life and glory (6.9.9).

This is a process of spiritual intimacy and illumination. We can be lured away from it, or momentarily distracted, but when we return to it, we continue on the path toward more and more profound intimacy and illumination. The light remains the light, unchanging, but we vary in how much we are distracted by and caught up in the materialistic and dualistic paradigm that is so prevalent. Gradual and sudden illumination are not therefore in opposition to one another, just different ways of understanding what underlies the alchemical process.

And what underlies the alchemical process, the *Emerald Tablet* tells us, is the power of all powers, permeating everything solid. It is present because it is inherent in everything even though it is not limited by anything. As such, it is the transcendence of separateness. William Law makes this clear in his version of Jacob Böhme's *Dialogues on the Supersensual Life*, where his master remarks, "Your own willing, hearing, and seeing hinder you from coming to the supersensual state. And it is because you strive against that out of which you yourself are derived that you separate yourself." We must arrive, his disciple says, "at this light above nature and creature."

We should observe here that the alchemical-gnostic perspective we are discussing is *not* denigrating the physical or natural world. Quite the opposite. It is saying that neither we nor nature are irredeemably fallen, but that rather through the alchemical process it is possible to restore both to the original unity that the primordial light reveals. The broader significance of this restoration of the human community is made visible in different alchemical illustrations, including those of *Splendor Solis*, which show a paradisal landscape and people. This is spiritual community in nature. To this theme we now turn.

PART FOUR
THE RED

10
Seeding New Cultures

Thus is everything created.
EMERALD TABLET

At some point, we began to realize that things have gone haywire. Before then, we could perhaps live in our bubble, telling ourselves that because our personal sphere was more or less comfortable and familiar, things were not so bad. But then the signs became clearer and clearer, and there were ever more of them—indicators that the jerry-rigged system of modernity, for all its technical prowess, was destined to fall apart. All composite things are by their very nature contingent and temporary. It is easy for us to believe in the permanence of our devices, of ourselves, of our friends and family, but whether we like it or not, all are ultimately contingent and temporary.

Great empires fall. It is in their nature. Sometimes they are sabotaged and rot from within, sometimes they are invaded, but usually it is a combination of the two. And empires are not cultures; they are a combination of vast wealth and power, exploitation, and good fortune with a centralized political organization that is guided with some cunning. It is possible to imagine an empire that protects individual cultures and peoples; the empire could be conceived as a shield for them.

But here we are considering cultures, a different matter. How do cultures emerge? What is a culture? And what role might alchemy have in helping us understand the answers to such questions? Alchemy is not necessarily only about individual alchemists and their laboratories, after all. We might be able to expand our alchemical perspective from the individual and the small group, to a culture. What is an alchemical understanding of what a culture is, how it emerges, and why?

PRIMORDIAL CULTURE AND THE FUTURE ARCHAIC

Let us say that a fallen society is the nigredo. The black. As we have discussed, this means decay, atomization, and materialism, meaning, also, nihilism. Exploitation, struggle, anxiety, fear, wrath . . . all are dominant. Such a society is opposed to spirituality, which rulers regard as threatening to the power of the state, or the power of whatever organization, criminal or otherwise, acts as a kind of state power. Authoritarian states can endure for some time, but eventually, however diabolically clever their rulers are, they will fall. We can envision all kinds of fallen societies, can't we?

Let us envision, after a future collapse, a post-apocalyptic world. Remnants of technology exist, of course, but the vast, complex systems of modernity largely do not. Huge urban sprawl is no more. The prodigious energy draw required by transportation and computer systems is no more. And nature begins to rebound, as it always does. Remaining humans perforce return to archaic ways of living—on small farms, in villages, fishing, hunting, and gathering. People band together for mutual protection, with local militia, local magistrates, a sheriff. Life is local.

How, in this post-apocalyptic world, does culture begin to emerge? Locally, then regionally. Directly connecting the natural, spiritual, and human realms in a particular landscape, among a particular people, and so also, tribally. Here we are discussing future archaic origins, so the word *archaic* doesn't connote the distant past, but rather carries the meaning of the Greek word *arche*, as in *archetype*, connoting primordial beginning, cause, or origin.

The *future archaic* may seem to be a contradiction in terms, but it is a way of describing and understanding primordial human life aligned with our natural, human, and spiritual flourishing. Culture emerges primordially—that is, out of renewed deep harmonious connections between these realms—so to understand its origin requires us to leave behind our preconceptions and conditioning to see things anew, in a new light.

Primordial culture is revealed; it is illuminated from beyond a solely human-centric materialistic perspective. In a primordial understanding, human beings, human families, and tribal groups are linked as clans with specific zoomorphic totems, such as an eagle, a trout, a badger. The animals are those of the particular landscape, and they are, of course, not only animals but also spiritual archetypes, understood as guides, helpers, and protectors.

Primordial culture is the fusion of the natural, human, and spiritual realms that in turn manifests in the dreams and tales of those who are called to be seers and storytellers. Of course, there is another dimension to the emergence of culture, beyond the imagination of any particular individual. The fusion of these three realms is what produces the shared cultural imagination to which others contribute, and that collectively begins to take on life, to grow, to spread, to become independently alive.

Out of this fusion emerges the living culture that manifests in epics, the shared stories of warriors and seers, of valiant heroes and heroines that emerge naturally from the character of the people and the landscape together, infused by their spiritual archetypes. Here, of course, we are looking not backward at the past but forward to the future archaic, at epics and shared stories and myths or folklore to come that will define the emergent culture.

This fusion we can call cultural alchemy. Cultural alchemy is produced by primordial illumination; that is, from an alchemical perspective, the alchemical process is revealing a primordial state of harmony and unity, and cultural alchemy is revealing in human life a distinctive way of understanding and realizing this primordial harmony in a particular landscape, in particular mountains, valleys, skies, and waters, among a particular people. Cultural alchemy thus bears the unique stamp of a particular region and a particular people.

But there is something beyond this unique stamp of a region or people also to bear in mind: its spiritual and transcendent origin. Unique colors mark particular peoples and areas, but beyond those unique colors is light itself, that which illuminates them. Illuminated culture means that there are those who are aware of and guide cultural alchemy, those who are aware that beyond the particular colors is the light that illuminates them.

In this context, the red stage is the alchemical flowering not only of an individual, or of a couple, but of a community that includes the spiritual, the natural, and the human together in union. The red is the stage of union, the transcendence of duality, and is represented in the philosopher's stone that heals and transmutes and with which we can flourish. The red stage is fullness, completion—it is restoration of the golden age.

In Buddhism, there is the word *enlightened*, or *enlightenment*, and we do find the word *illumined*, or *illumination*, in Christian mysticism, which is somewhat close to *enlightenment* in Buddhism. Western European history includes the term *illuminati*, but this term and its essentially politicomagical implications, despite the apparent prominence of light in it, has little or nothing to do with cultural alchemy as understood here. An enlightened culture is one that encourages and serves the shared aim of spiritual awakening and illumination.

Is there a word for those who transmit the light? The ancient tradition, which we see reflected in Orphism, was initiatic, meaning that someone who experienced illumination in turn passed that on to another, who in turn passed it on to another. Someone *initiates* the transmission, and it continues through generations, ending only when, for whatever reason, it is not passed on.

We have been conditioned, in modernity, to think of *culture* as a generic term for almost anything in secular, materialistic human society, so people refer to "pop culture," to "corporate culture," and so forth, as if culture was the same as society, but the word *culture* actually has the root *cultus*, meaning cultivation or caring for, including cultivation, caring for, or devotion to the divine. Culture is caring for, creating, participating in, encouraging, and connecting the human, natural, and divine realms. It means continuing and participating in a fully balanced, harmonious way of being that recognizes and respects all three realms.

Culture, then, manifests as harmonious balance between the human, natural, and divine realms, which are deeply interwoven and permeate one another. If culture is dissociated from the natural world, from plants, animals, and the deep lore of the rhythms of nature, then it is not culture in any meaningful sense. If culture is disconnected from the spiritual realm, then it is also not culture in any profound sense. Culture cannot be confined to only the human or only the human and natural realms.

Modernity represents the breaking of limits and boundaries, and is antihuman, antinatural, and antispiritual in its most toxic forms, which we see in communism but also in corporationism as well as in "transhumanist" technocracy. Modernity in its most extreme form is totalitarian, brooking no dissenting views and seeking to alter and erase our most deeply human, natural, and divine elements in order to impose a reductionistic, barren worldview on everyone. We see this in "cultural revolutions" that seek to overthrow social order, to destroy religious tradition, to denigrate and eliminate the past and all that is meaningful in human life. Cultural revolution is the negation of authentic culture.

What does a healthy culture look like? What makes it truly healthy and aligned with natural and human limits? Such a culture has a divinely illuminated center. It is oriented toward spiritual illumination and freedom, and it is not focused only on manipulation, domination, and exploitation of the natural world as "resources." It is not focused on imposing political dogmas on others, punishing dissidents, and enforcing a secular authoritarian hegemony while encouraging the exploitation and destruction of nature. A healthy culture oriented toward spiritual illumination looks completely different from this.

HEALTHY CULTURES OF THE PAST AND PRESENT

We do have examples of healthy established cultures in the recent past and in the present. Often they are found in mountainous regions, in part because mountains make conquest more difficult and protect the cultures so that they can develop generationally over millennia. Here I am not idealizing any culture—of course, we can find problems in any human society. But there are clearly examples of cultures that can be recognized as models.

In the Himalayas, we have multiple examples of profound and balanced cultures that incorporate an alchemical, transmutative perspective and are oriented toward spiritual illumination, awakening. I say multiple examples because culture is local and regional, so even though Buddhism is predominant, there are countless local flowerings, including Bön, and we are reflecting here on how that local, nascent dimension emerges.

In Tibet, before the Chinese Communist invasion and occupation, there were numerous regional and local traditions and practices, and though some of these survived the sustained Chinese efforts to suppress and obliterate them, much has been lost. But what has been largely lost did survive and continue in Bhutan, that quixotic Buddhist kingdom in the Himalayas that remains so culturally rich, and somewhat, though not completely, protected from the depredations of the outside world.

Bhutan has its own distinctive history, traditions, and applications of Buddhism, as well as shamanic traditions under the name Bön. The relationships between Buddhism and Bön are too complex to delve into here, so a better way might be to discuss transcendent and immanent traditions. Transcendent traditions are focused as the name suggests on metaphysical transcendence, enlightenment, and liberation. Immanent or cosmological traditions are concerned with human, natural, and spiritual flourishing.

We find both in Buddhism, but we also can find in Bhutan the coexistence of Buddhist transcendent traditions with Bön traditions focused on cosmological aims like restoring vitality or prosperity. It's not that these aren't also addressed in Buddhism; it's just that in practice, one can find Buddhism and Bön coexisting.

Bhutan exists in the ambit of Tibetan Buddhism, of course, yet also has its own unique and legendary figures, some of whom exemplify crazy wisdom, like Drukpa Kunley, a wild yogi in the Mahamudra tradition of Saraha, who composed many ribald songs and is said to have inspired the practice of adorning and protecting buildings or sacred places with images of erect phalluses, the archaic symbol of fertility, flourishing, and protection.

The point here is not to impose a particular Bhutanese model on a place but rather to recognize that living culture can be ribald and futuristically archaic, irreverent and deeply reverent at the same time, humorous and sincere at once—and as diverse as are human beings and their environments. Bhutanese cultures, like Tibetan, share their central orientation on the Buddhist path of enlightenment, but the local applications are richly diverse.

This richness can include vast libraries and universities, such as Nalanda. It can include monasteries and spiritual centers with ordained monastics. It can include local ngakpas, or lay practitioners with families, working to help their locale and its people and beings flourish. And it can include also wild yogis and solitary recluses devoted to spiritual practice and illumination.

In the titular chapter of my book *The Mystical State*, I discuss Nicholas von Flue, a patron saint of Swiss culture, known colloquially as Brother Klaus. He lived his life in a valley in central Switzerland and later in life became a hermit, like some Tibetan yogis, famous for not needing food and for giving blessings and advice in the region. He is credited for saving the Switzerland confederation from civil war, and when you are in his valley, you can feel that it is a special place, known still as the Ranft.

Cultures are oriented toward spiritual illumination and toward human, natural, and spiritual flourishing. They recognize that our human purpose in life is not selfish acquisition and exploitation, not outside ourselves in "virtual reality" or some other mirage, not achieved by clearcutting forests and mining in vast pits or by despoliation, but by honoring an inner spiritual life that recognizes the beauty and inestimable value of the natural world around us and seeks to create and sustain harmony with it and with the spirits and invisible beings that surround us.

ENVISIONING HARMONIOUS NEW CULTURES

Seeing new cultures means germinating them, first through vision. Looking ahead, bearing alchemy in mind, we can envision a harmonious way of being that is oriented toward and by spiritual illumination that unites humanity and nature through culture. Culture is integrative spirituality manifested in the human and natural worlds. Culture reveals the spiritual dimensions of nature and humanity.

Many assume that culture is a purely human creation, but this kind of thinking derives from a materialistic bias that excludes spirituality and the spiritual dimensions of humanity and nature. The integrative unity of the spiritual, human, and natural is expressed in archaic cultures through kinship—people are born from the union of or from gods, and their heraldic insignia convey their spiritual connection to nature, to archetypal animals, birds, or fishes, sometimes in mythical form. Family lineage is consanguine with all three realms.

We need new terms and a new way of understanding cultural alchemy. A materialistic worldview is a dead end and cannot provide any basis for understanding cultural alchemy. Only an open perspective that incorporates a transcendent understanding of humanity and nature or an understanding that humanity and nature are translucent to the spiritual realm provides the basis for cultural alchemy. To describe this for a new time, new terms are needed.

An important concept here is *primordialism*. Primordialism for us means restoring our original nature, returning to an archaic balance of all three realms, a return to origins and so also a return to eternity, or timelessness. All new cultures are primordial, meaning that they reflect their eternal origin and meaning; they are closer to eternity. The purpose of alchemy is a return to the primordial condition of both humanity and nature, symbolized by the philosopher's stone. Cultural alchemy means a shared renewal of humanity's and nature's primordial state.

Primordialism is a comprehensive concept and doesn't refer only to linguistic or ethnic origins. It is not enough to rectify this or that aspect of fallen society gone awry when the whole is entirely off kilter and destined for collapse. This is how we naturally think: things would be more or less all right if only we could fix x or y. But fixing x or y is not the answer. Primordialism is much more comprehensive than fixing only this or that particular problem—it is the result and also the origin of cultural alchemy. Cultural alchemy emerges from and results in primordiality. This is what is meant in the *Emerald Tablet* by "thus is everything created." Alchemy is the process of creation and recreation, of purification, illumination, and union, or restoration. It is the creative process inherent in nature and in us. It is and reveals the primordial. What that means is the subject of our next chapter.

11
Restoring Wholeness and Flourishing

From here proceed wonderful adaptations, of which this is the process.

Emerald Tablet

As the *Emerald Tablet* asserts above, "From here proceed wonderful adaptations, of which this is the process." This observation exactly corresponds to our larger theme of cultural alchemy. It refers to multiple "adaptations" of the process—why? Because the adaptation of the alchemical light process is decentralized; it takes place individually, in couples, in small groups, in tribes or families, in localities and regions, in each case uniquely according to circumstances. The genius of alchemy is that it provides the template or process, but it is up to us to realize it in our own circumstances.

While one must pursue the alchemical light path individually, what is often overlooked is this larger context of cultural creation and transformation without which one remains an isolated individual seeking to assist in larger cultural awakening but without a clear context for understanding what that means, let alone for bringing it about. This larger context, and with it intention and aspiration, is vital for the future.

Of course, it was common among those who recognized what was happening to our society to observe that we were caught in the throes of a decline into a dark age, and this was true, but it also was too pessimistic. Recognizing that we are at the end of an age allows us to look toward the beginning of the next one. And that is really what we are doing here by looking at cultural alchemy and primordialism.

Primordialism helps us understand who we are and what optimal culture looks like in a completely new and transformed, holistic way. Primordialism (a way of describing the red stage) provides a much vaster vision because it proceeds from new and ancient archaic premises. To realize it, we must begin by giving up our illusions. We must give up the lies that we have been told and that we have told ourselves. We must let go of our preconceptions and our self-righteous posturing, our delusional constructs, to begin to see things anew and holistically.

The hardest part of one's journey is the nigredo. In a time like ours, nigredo means the breaking down and jettisoning of illusions. We cling to the falsehoods we've been told, and it is hard to find our way unaided past them to what is true and enduring, especially when the system around us actively censors and propagandizes itself. But as we begin to awaken, we also see that there are others who are also awakening. These are our companions on the journey, our spiritual family.

SPIRITUAL FAMILIES

There are two kinds of spiritual family. One is our tribe, the people into which we were born and to whom we have ancestral debts and connections. Totalitarian systems want to ignore and erase this tribal spiritual family and to atomize us into separated individuals without any deeper connections. But these deeper connections are where authentic culture originates and flowers. When you are born into a particular family and region, you have hidden connections to the landscape, the waters, and the sky in that place. Culture is that which links the human, the natural, and the spiritual realms so that all can flourish.

Culture, in this deep, primordial sense is perpetually being renewed as generations pass. Culture is dynamic stability. A lucid culture is universal but particular to people and place even as light itself is universal, yet manifests uniquely in particular places. The sharp light in Cornwall is different from the light elsewhere, just as the new world light on a bay in Costa Rica is different than light elsewhere. A lucid culture in the way we are describing it here is localized, unique.

The other kind of spiritual family is of the heart. It is elective affinity. We feel called. The Buddhist word is *sangha*, which hearkens back to the Indo-European root word *sem* meaning "as one," "together with," or "like." Of course, it can include our tribal family members, but this spiritual family is one to which we are called; we join it consciously, not through birth alone. And it is profoundly spiritual. Its origins are transcendent and by joining it, we enter into its community.

Both kinds of family are essential in a living culture. We need to understand that machine society, with its totalizing materialism and antinatural and antispiritual dogmas, is antithetical to a lucid culture. It is possible to live in a machine society and affirm a lucid culture both tribal and spiritual, but only through a conscious, sustained effort. When there are others of like mind, this creates an island culture.

ISLAND CULTURE

What does such an island culture look like? It is holistic, affirming all three realms. It affirms primordial nature, primordial humanity, and primordial spirituality. If it rejects one or more of these, then it is not really a culture in the sense we are describing here. A religion that rejects the Pagan folk traditions of nature and nature spirits, and whose adherents regard the natural world as a collection of resources to be exploited, cannot animate a healthy living culture. A society that rejects one's ancestral inheritance and atomizes people is fundamentally antihuman. A lucid culture respects all three realms.

Where can examples of such cultures be found? One is in Ireland, where you see the fusion, or at least, the shared existence of Christian and ancient Pagan traditions, in what is often called Celtic Christianity. Another is Bhutan, where we see the similarly sometimes fraught coexistence of Vajrayana Buddhism and the Pagan religion of Bön, with its rituals for placating local nature spirits, finding lost parts of one's soul, or shamanic healing, and other aspects of pragmatic folk religion. Still another is in Bali, where local traditions continue, especially in the wild mountains and remoter areas but even in towns and cities.

In such traditions, we can see the intersection of transcendent and immanent religion. In Christianity, transcendent religion is represented by apophatic mysticism, the current that we see from Dionysius the Areopagite and his *Mystical Theology* through Irish spiritual author John Scotus Eriugena and German mystic Meister Eckhart to Jacob Böhme. Immanent religion is represented in Celtic Christianity in the continuity of Pagan or folk traditions concerning the faeries, the otherworld, and the secrets of nature and of spirits. And the ancient megalithic monuments are present throughout Ireland.

The archaic traditions of megalithic stones include all three realms: natural, human, and spiritual. The stones are, of course, in and of nature, marking sacred places in the landscape, but they are also directly tied to the human realm through ancestral or funereal practices, and they are linked also to the spirit realm or otherworld. So too, an ancestral practice of giving an offering to local spirits or nonphysical beings connects humans, nature, and spirits.

What connects all of these ultimately is light, first literally, as when the stones are placed to mark the solstice or equinox or the solar or lunar cycles, and as when offerings are given at certain times, such as morning or evening, the coming or going of light. But also figuratively, as these archaic cultural traditions are about the light of consciousness. The standing stone rising above the Earth is a pillar representing the movement of consciousness from below to above, and from above to below. And an offering of milk and dough is saying "I recognize you are here" or "I am conscious of you." It shows respect.

How particular cultures manifest themselves obviously varies widely. What I am suggesting here are broad commonalities, the principles informing them, without which a culture does not really exist at all. Essential to culture is consciousness, conscious recognition of ancestors, those who have gone before, consciousness of nature and of nature spirits, consciousness also of our own effort to go from darkness toward illumination and freedom. A culture is a healthy collective home, in harmony with nature, that encourages spiritual growth toward awakening. The red stage can be understood as the flowering of such a culture.

Such a lucid island culture is possible now and always. Of course, it does not require a literal island, as the term is metaphorical, referring to a culture that develops independently from the surrounding society, whatever that may look like. But an island does mean separation by a graceful distance of miles. The great Mystery center on the island of Samothrace required an initiatory journey just to reach it, and perhaps that is the case with all such spiritual centers. I discuss this in *Entering the Mysteries: The Secret Traditions of Indigenous Europe*. Another sacred island is Olkhon—in Lake Baikal, the vast freshwater ocean—with its sacred cave, Shaman's Rock, and other sacred sites.

In *The Secret Island*, I discuss not only literal islands, including, of course, that home of many mysteries, Ireland, and places as far-flung as Taiwan and Hawaii, but also metaphorical islands of living myth where the Grail tradition is still alive. Such places become more alive the more you are aware of their mythic dimensions embedded in the landscape, waters, and air. To walk in such a place is to be in two worlds at once: the one you see and the secret world of myth.

These places signal to us what an authentic, living culture is: a synergetic union of the spiritual, human, and natural worlds. This union means the flourishing of both the human and natural worlds. But each landscape and each people who belong to and in it are unique and precious. We can think of countless such places, from the Grail landscape of Brittany to the high hills of Ireland, from remote valleys in Nepal or Bhutan to wherever you are as you read this. Hence the *Emerald Tablet*'s assertion that "from here," that is, from each unique place and people, "proceed wonderful adaptations, of which this is the process."

The "wonderful adaptions" of cultural creation are like light passing into a precious stone, producing distinctive colors and patterns. The light is the spiritual source, passing into this world through the visionary or revealer figure that inaugurates a new cultural cycle. There is something inherently mysterious about this process, and, of course, not all cultures are the same, nor are all sources the same. Some are profoundly kind, others harsh, depending on the spiritual source, the people, and the place.

In Tibetan Buddhism, there is a tradition of what are called "hidden lands," *beyuls* in Tibetan. This is the origin of what became known as the imaginary realm of Shangri-La and the most well-known mythical kingdom of Shambhala. The hidden lands are protected realms, where spiritual practitioners can thrive and awaken despite the hostile, degenerated world outside. They are said to have their own royalty, their own people, and their own natural environment, rather like the faery realm in Western Europe.

Rather than going on a wild goose chase for a hidden land somewhere else, here we are turning to the spiritual dimensions of where we are now. The myth of Shambhala is powerful and has an archaic resonance; it reminds us of what authentic living culture is and how we can move toward living in it, not as an exotic place somewhere far off, but where we find ourselves now.

PLACES OF WHOLENESS AND FLOURISHING

What characterizes a place of wholeness and flourishing? There are so many different aspects to this, across the full spectrum of human and natural life: songs, poems, stories, plays, spiritual epics, and theater—the elements of new literature at the dawn of a new cultural age; medicine that heals both humans and animals through knowledge of plant and mineral secrets; metallurgy and the other plastic creative arts, such as sculpture and ceramics; agriculture in deep synergy with the hidden cycles of the natural world, spiritually blessed; other crafts that draw from the local natural world; mythology that manifests the profound hidden links between the human, natural, and spiritual realms; and above all, religion that encourages kindness, wisdom, and spiritual awakening.

The Hermetic tradition calls us back to archaic, profound spiritual archetypes for human life lived in deep harmony with the natural world, back to our origins and purpose. We have forgotten all these, distracted as we are by the illusory gewgaws of modern technology with its seductive artifices. But as soon as we remember them, we remember our authentic calling. Heed that longing for what is true and real.

Even if we find ourselves living in a time when, as the great poet William Butler Yeats put it, "things fall apart; the centre cannot hold," still it is possible to fix our eye on cultural creation. On this, too, alchemy has much to offer. Usually alchemy is presented as an individual process, and of course, it is that. But here we begin to see that it is a cosmic process of regeneration that also has broader implications for human community.

The need for this cultural regeneration actually was forecast by Guru Rinpoche, the founding archetypal figure of Tibetan Buddhism, who lived in the eighth century. He said that in the future, there would come a time when the five poisons (ignorance, attachment, anger, jealousy, and pride) would permeate society, and everything would disintegrate around us. Beyond the obvious cultural disintegration, there would come the actual persecution of spiritual people. During this period, religious monuments, spiritual teachings, including books, and spiritual teachers would be proscribed and practitioners imprisoned and killed. When these things happen, he said, you should build religious monuments (stupas) and retreat centers, and go on pilgrimages because these kinds of activities can delay the decline around you.

But eventually you will need to get out of the deteriorating, toxic society and find your way to a new and renewed community in a new place. In this new place, which can be understood as a "hidden land" (*beyul*), you should create new religious monuments and dharma centers, and generate a new community of spiritual practitioners. While in the outer world there is darkness, chaos, and disintegration, in this special place, under Padmasambhava's protection, a virtuous refuge community of light can be sustained.

You can see hints of an analogous vision in some alchemical images, where the landscape and people are integrated into a harmonious whole under the glow of restored solar and lunar light. There is a reason that alchemical images emphasize the king and the queen, and why in traditional societies both Eastern and Western, you find a monarch. Just because contemporary ideology frowns on this does not invalidate it when the right circumstances appear. The figures of a king and a queen, visible in so much alchemical imagery, are deep and archaic and have a primordial resonance. The king and the queen may or may not be literally present in order to be at the center of culture; the king and queen represent and evoke the archetypal center out of which culture emerges and is sustained.

The *Emerald Tablet* points to the process of creation itself, which is also the process of rebirth and restoration. From here come "wonderful adaptations" of the process—meaning that the alchemical process is not only individual, not only that of a divine couple, but also that of community and of emergent cultures. But each culture, in a unique place, with a unique people, is itself unique, a wonderful adaptation to the particularities of a landscape and a people.

An alchemical vision helps us orient ourselves in a confusing and confused society; it reminds us of the enduring truths of who we are as human beings, and how we can flourish. This flourishing involves not only an individual but a group and community; it is beyond us as individuals. It is not only about us. It is about what lies beyond us, in the spiritual, natural, and human worlds restored to their primordial freshness.

12
A Vision

> *Therefore I am called Hermes Trismegistus, having the three parts of the philosophy of the whole world.*
> *That which I had to say concerning the operation of the Sun is completed.*
>
> — EMERALD TABLET

In the epigraph above are the lines that conclude the *Emerald Tablet*. But what does "therefore I am called Hermes Trismegistus, having the three parts of the philosophy of the whole world" mean? The term *trismegistus* means "thrice-greatest," and the lines are spoken by Hermes, the messenger god. What are the three parts of the philosophy of the whole world? There are different ways to understand this, of course, but one is the three parts to which we have already referred: human, natural, and spiritual. These three realms all intersect in the alchemical process in which the human and natural realms are restored to their primordial perfection. Philosophy, the love of wisdom, is here not simply analytical, or rational, or materialistic—it is the knowledge that transmutes, that reveals spiritual reality.

Who is Hermes? Among the ancient gods, he is the one who crosses the boundaries between the human and divine realms; hence he is known as the messenger. He is the forerunner; the one who invented the lyre, hence music, and the alphabet, hence writing. He invented dice and is therefore the patron of luck, and he is shown sometimes with a purse, as the patron of trade. He is also the patron of rural areas and shepherds. He is the father of the pastoral god Pan, and the guide of the souls of the dead in the afterlife. He is a patron of homes; hence in the ancient world families' homes often featured his stone monument by the doorway. And in the ancient countryside, you will find herms, or stone pillars, in the fields, marking the crossing of boundaries. Hermes, guide of souls, is the kindly mentor who consecrates the landscape for those who live in it and travel through it. Hermes is patron of primordial human and natural flourishing.

And what does it mean that what he has to say of the "operation of the Sun" is completed? The "operation of the Sun" refers to the alchemical process of transmutation and illumination. In the culmination of the alchemical process, we see in the alchemical illustrations, the Sun illuminates the heart of the regenerated man. In the red stage, the planets are restored to their original, unfallen nature in relation to the Sun. And in some alchemical manuscripts, you see an unfallen, pristine landscape and people illuminated by a golden Sun and silvery Moon. The king and the queen are restored to their rightful place.

This restoration is also visible in the Grail tradition, as we will recall. The Grail quest moves from a fallen to a restored kingdom. How is a kingdom restored? Through continuity. The knight and his lady are tested, he undergoes the quest, they become the royal couple, and the kingdom is renewed in its primordial resplendence. A generational transition and regeneration takes place. Of course, this can be understood as an individual or couple's journey, but it is also that of a community. The macrocosm mirrors the microcosm; the king and queen *are* the community.

It was only a moment ago, historically, when this coinherence of the ruler and the kingdom was natural. It was lost for a time. But, inherent in human nature, it recurs. If we are born into a bureaucratic era of regulations and policies, of laws and administrative edicts, or an oligarchy misleadingly presented as the result of "democracy," or the "will of the people," it may take us some time to leave behind our conditioning. But we are reminded of the primordial when we look at alchemical images of regenerated culture. We are reminded of what is natural in the most profound sense.

To understand the primordial, we have to shed our layers of preconceptions and see things anew. We can see things anew through initiatory literature, sometimes called fairy tales, sometimes epic poems or songs, sometimes myths, sometimes romances. It is a sign of the fallen times in which you live if these are dismissed or discredited and not recognized for their power and meaning. Initiatory literature, whether it be the epics of Homer or those of the Tibetan Gesar of Ling, orients and guides us, showing us how to live. They encode spiritual truth.

FAIRY TALES AS INITIATORY LITERATURE

Fairy tales are initiatory literature, not quite religious, yet not secular, in that liminal space that includes both and is neither. Fairy tales convey archaic Pagan or magical folk knowledge, and the root history of the word fairy—fae, fée, or fay—is revealing. These words convey very interesting and provocative meanings. The word fae has the same root as fate, fated, or the fates. It also shares its Indo-European root meaning "to speak" with fame, fable, prophet, and prophetic, and it is linked also with ban, meaning "proclamation." All of these words linked together form a pattern that allows us to begin to see more deeply what a fairy tale is. While the term "fairy tale" is familiar, its cognate is the word "faery," which refers not only to children's tales, but to a different kind of being hidden in nature.

The word *faery* connotes an enchanted domain, a magical realm inhabited as a separate faery kingdom. The faery kingdom is supernatural, meaning that it exists both within and beyond the natural world, in a kind of twilight zone where time passes differently than in our swiftly changing physical world. Folklore says that those humans who enter this intermediate world may discover that decades or even centuries have passed in the human world while they were in the faery realm. Hearing or reading a faery tale means we are in touch with this otherworldly kingdom.

Faery tales are, in the Old English, *wyrd*. The word *wyrd* gives us the word *weird*, but that conveys only some of the meaning. *Wyrd* refers to what "turns out," what is fated to be, or what the goddesses of fate decree. It has the same root as the German word *werden*, meaning "to become," from the root *wer*, meaning "to turn, or bend." But *wyrd* also conveys that which is supernatural, or uncanny, or surreal. The faery tale unites all of these implications into one: fated, fate, fame, fable, prophet, prophetic, the *wyrd*, that which turns out or turns into, transforms, becomes, that which is worthy. In this single word, *wyrd*, so much is conveyed.

Irish folk respect and fear the fairies, called sidhe, pronounced "shee." From this root comes the word *banshee*, of which you might have heard. On one of my travels in Ireland, I encountered an elderly innkeeper who told me folk wisdom and stories about the sidhe from his childhood. He said that they travel on the wind, and when a particular kind of sidhe wind rises, it's best to just lay flat on the ground and let it pass over. And you'd best hope you do not hear the frightening cry of the banshee announcing death in the family. Almost every story he told conveyed a sense of caution, if not outright fear.

This same sense of recognized power extends to the landscape itself. A sacred landscape, with its high crags, its caves, its lakes and rushing waters, is numinous, which means it has power. It is inhabited not only by people or animals but also by other beings with otherworldly power for good or for ill. Power to bless means power to curse, and numinous power can be unpredictable. If you attune to a particular being associated with a locality or region, you may encounter it, but your engagement may be terrifying.

This numinous power permeates fairy tales worthy of the name, and it is also what protects the hidden land or local realm. It is what empowers sacred speech, the root meaning behind *fae* and its affiliated words like *prophetic*. Really, the hidden land is in some sense *spoken* into being. Those not meant for it are *banned* from entering it. It is *wyrd* not in an abstract or remote way but in a real and present way. To enter it is to enter into a different realm where obdurate dualistic materialism does not hold sway any longer.

THE INITIATE'S JOURNEY AND THE MUTUALLY TRANSFORMATIVE PATH

Either you are outside or you are within the initiatory realm. One or the other. There is the exoteric—those outside—and the esoteric, those who have entered. To enter or to be born into the realm and to have passed certain thresholds is to be an initiate or, in verb form, to initiate, that is, to begin one's inner journey. There are those who have not begun that journey, and those who have.

From the outside, one can make all kinds of judgments, assertions, even wild claims, but the truth is that from the outside, one has no real knowledge, only a combination of hearsay and speculation. Obdurate dualist materialists want to lay sole claim to authority, but ironically, they least of all have authority in such matters. And on some level, they know it. That's why they act as they do, often acting like a child throwing a tantrum when they don't get their way.

But you know better. Perhaps you're already an initiate, that is, you've begun the journey in earnest. Initiating your journey means that you've entered into sacred space, as we put it in our Hieros Institute website. You've passed the herms that mark the sacred space; you've felt the presence of the invisible; you know that nature is not just a collection of dead objects or "resources" but is alive, and in it spirits are present.

Wouldn't it be wonderful to live in a community dedicated to such an understanding? To be among others who share ancestral and spiritual continuity? To live in an ever-deepening connection with the landscape and world around us? To be among those who share an alchemical understanding of a mutually transformative path? This is not just a pipe dream, though it is that too. It is also inevitable.

Inevitable because the alchemical transformative path reflects how nature, humanity, and the spiritual really are. It reflects the profound and archaic perennial truth of what we are capable of becoming. Human and natural and spiritual flourishing are intrinsic to who we are and where we are. Our knowledge of the hidden aspects of nature is insight into nature's perennial secrets, and the principles of natural healing are intrinsic to our human condition in the natural world imbued with spiritual vitality.

Understand: this is a vision of a particular kind of path and a community. It can exist irrespective of what is happening elsewhere; it exists on its own terms with a folk in a particular landscape. For this reason, it is pragmatic and realizable in our time and in the time to come. It is not a projected vision of a greater illumination of or revelation for all people everywhere, not at all. Rather, it is vision, seeing a locus for living culture.

ELEMENTS OF AN EMERGENT CULTURE

What are the elements of this emergent culture in this particular locus among this particular folk? Let us reflect on them, not necessarily in order of importance but just as observations. First, there is a collectively recognized transmutational path, an alchemical path that is affirmed by the community. Its specific orientation depends on the life inclination of those there. It may be Nyingma Buddhist, it may be Christian gnostic, it may be Pagan, or it may be Taoist. But a transformative path is essential. This is a shared commitment to mutually encouraged waking up.

Second, we need to recognize elders and guides. An elder is not simply someone who is older. It is someone with life wisdom. This is directly related to the transmutational path. On such a path, there are those with more experience and understanding, those who know more clearly the dangers and the direction best taken, the process and the stages of it. These are the beacons in the community of light. Eastern Orthodox Christianity in some branches continued the ancient tradition of spiritual elders and guides, but most branches of Christianity as a whole lost track of it. And who speaks of sages these days? Yet sages are much needed. We need a community of light that produces and recognizes sages.

In Tibetan Buddhist culture, early on there developed a tradition of the ngakpas, lay practitioners who could marry and have children, and who could serve as a kind of local shaman and spiritual resource in the village or locality. People would know to come to the ngakpa for practical advice and to help positively resolve life challenges. This, or something like this, follows naturally from the idea of elders and sages and is a vital aspect of the light community, for there is someone who can bring to bear ancient wisdom in daily life.

Third, there is a deep understanding of the natural world and how to work with it. The light community recognizes that there are hidden dimensions to nature, and that farming, hunting, gathering, fishing, herbal healing work, and so much more all need to work with the profound harmonic patterns in nature and in us. Astrology provides us with keys to understanding those inner patterns, which are not only inherent in our own psyche but also are woven through our path of transformation and the natural world.

Fourth, we need to recognize the necessity for a community library, a shared collection of profound and practical wisdom that is combined with the community school. A library's purpose is not to collect everything, certainly not to collect harmful or misleading works, but rather to house what is most valuable for the light community. Such a community includes in its library the classics of mysticism, works by Dionysius the Areopagite, Plotinus, and the other Platonists, *Periphyseon*, *The Cloud of Unknowing*, and other works (including classical works of Tibetan Buddhism) that illuminate the nature of consciousness.* It includes works on herbalism, agriculture, botany, zoology, astrology, and classical literature.

Fifth, the light community emphasizes initiatory life paths, which can take the form of guilds. Guilds are an ancient idea whose time is always now. There can be in guilds many callings, some traditional like

---

*For an overview of this Western tradition, see Arthur Versluis, *Platonic Mysticism*.

carpentry, masonry, building, or farming, others newer, such as electrical, electronic, or other kinds of technological work. What distinguishes them is that guilds encourage spiritually enlivened callings that regard work as part of the path.

These are indications of a larger perspective into which technology is incorporated and subsumed. Of course, it is possible to go the direction of the Amish or Mennonites, but even they incorporate some technology on their own terms. For instance, where I live, there are Amish communities in the region, and you encounter them occasionally in the local supermarket, driven there by someone with a van. It's true they don't have electricity or televisions in their houses, but they and the Mennonites have created ways to use some technology, while keeping the technological system subsumed.

The underlying principle in all these is continuing community integrity and higher purpose. Without these, or as these are eroded in modernity, as we have seen around the world, culture literally disintegrates. If all of the elements mentioned here dissolve—including the impelling spiritual purpose, of course, but also respect for elders, recognition of spiritual dimensions of nature, guilds, and so on—if everything falls apart, what is left if and when the vast supply chains of technological systems fail? Nothing, or nearly nothing. Higher shared purpose—flourishing and liberation—is not last, but first.

VESSELS FOR FUTURE CIVILIZATION

Light communities can be understood as vessels for future civilization; they can be seen as containing the vital seeds of renaissance, which means "rebirth." What is born anew is perennial, archaic, and primordial—terms that at least indicate the essential meaning here. For us to be fully human, we need to have a path and people who share that path with us from the past, in the present, and in the future. It is possible to intentionally create communities that understand themselves to be vessels into the future.

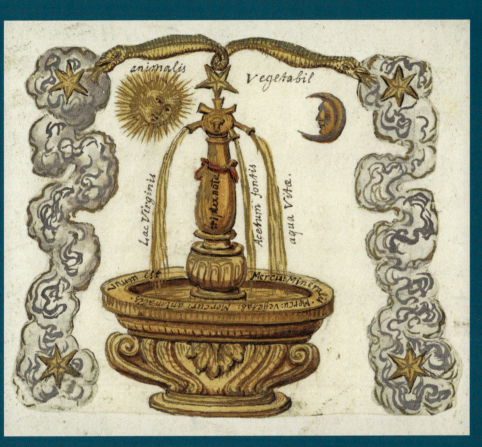

Plate 1. Fountain of life.
Ferguson Manuscript 210, image number 1.
With permission of University of Glasgow Archives & Special Collections.

Plate 2. The king and queen personify the Sun and Moon.
Ferguson Manuscript 210, image number 2.
With permission of University of Glasgow Archives & Special Collections.

Plate 3. The nude king and queen (Sun and Moon) become husband and wife.

Ferguson Manuscript 210, image number 3.
With permission of University of Glasgow Archives & Special Collections.

Plate 4. The nude king and queen intertwined.
Ferguson Manuscript 210, image number 11.
With permission of University of Glasgow Archives & Special Collections.

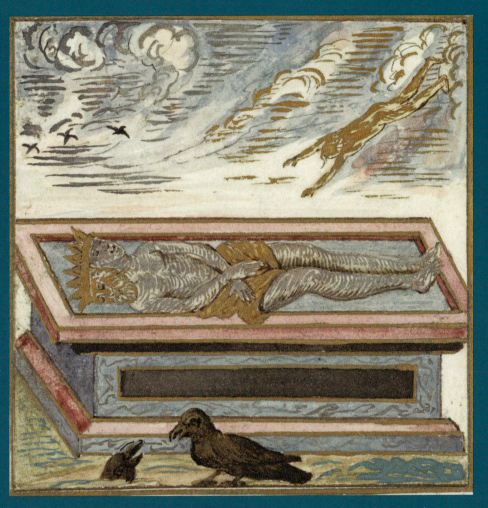

Plate 5. The king and queen join to become a single androgyne being.
Ferguson Manuscript 210, image number 9.
With permission of University of Glasgow Archives & Special Collections.

Plate 6. The king and queen transform into a resplendent winged androgyne.

Ferguson Manuscript 210, image number 10.
With permission of University of Glasgow Archives & Special Collections.

Plate 7. The process culminates in an angelic being representing illumination.
Ferguson Manuscript 210, image number 12.
With permission of University of Glasgow Archives & Special Collections.

Plate 8. The resurrected Christ above the opened grave.
Ferguson Manuscript 210, image number 20.
With permission of University of Glasgow Archives & Special Collections.

From late antiquity through the medieval period into modernity we find instances where such communities have been created. Hermetic, Gnostic, Pagan, Platonic, Transcendentalist, Brotherhood of the New Life, Distributist, Kibbo Kift, Lebensreformist, and hippie all come to mind, and all are social experiments of differing political alliances and varying longevity and success. The point here isn't to extol any of these but rather to say that such communities and movements have a long history that points to the idea of a renewed, primordial, and transformative community as an alchemical vessel for the future.

Here, we're reflecting not on erstwhile utopian experiments but on the deeper aspects of what drives living culture, what is vital in human life—how to not just live, but thrive. How can we incorporate into our shared lives the deeper elements of what it means to be fully human? Alchemy and the Hermetic tradition provide guideposts or herms that mark a transformative path, both for us and, potentially, for others too. But each of us is unique, and each community is unique, in the particular ways of realizing one's authentic nature in that place and time.

There is an alchemy of community. There is mystery in how culture emerges, just as there is mystery in the alchemical process. Both ultimately are about transmutation, about how if the right circumstantial preparation is there, along with right intention and careful attention, something miraculous can happen. Alchemy provides us with a transformational cartography, a way of understanding the larger process in light of its end or purpose. This is a way of understanding not only individual but also community transfiguration.

None of this is meant to suggest some vast social transfiguration and a new age in which typically one's spiritual aspiration is projected externally and imagined to take place out there, collectively, without our own spiritual work. If a prophesied grand golden age were to dawn upon us, well, great. But here we are reflecting on the flowering of small, decentralized, unique light communities, and such an endeavor can happen where we are now. It is not perpetually deferred after a failed prophetic date; it is a matter of shared spiritual purpose among like-minded people, expressed in your particular circumstances.

Such communities have appeared before. An example is visible in a spiritual memoir by Thomas Bromley titled *The Way to the Sabbath of Rest*. Bromley belonged to a spiritual community centered in the tradition of Jacob Böhme that flourished in the latter half of the seventeenth century in England. Note that a longer version of this extract can be found in the "Selected Readings" section at the end of the book.

Bromley writes of what it is like to be in a spiritually united community, in which:

> the further opening of those enjoyments, which flow from union with new relations . . . come now to be very dear, because the ground of the relation is so pure and good, being not of man, but of God. Here we shall experience the happy effects of our pure union, which produces that divine love that none can know, but those that enjoy it. But this will be strongest, where there is most harmony and agreement in spirits and natures; because the eternal tincture works upon and through everything according to its nature and capacity. Hence we come to enjoy more from some, than others; and some from us receive more than others. But that brotherly love and friendship, which now comes to be renewed in spirit, far transcends any enjoyments merely natural.

Bromley movingly recounts the joy and mutual love shared by those in the community, who would gladly surrender their own happiness to relieve another's suffering in the group. What is more, Bromley gives us indications of how and why this alchemical community flourished. Its community was not physical, but metaphysical, beyond the apparent limits of time and space. In it, they experienced:

> pure love, which is not affection, but something above it; not consisting in sudden outflowings and eruptions, but in a constant sweet inclination and secret propensity of the spirit, to those which are one with it,

in the pure life. And this good-willingness is so great that from it the soul could give its life (or if there were anything dearer than life) for its brother; and choose sufferings, to free others from them. In this state there will be a sympathizing in joy and sorrow; and where the union is eminently great, there may be some knowledge of each others' conditions at a distance, which comes from their being essenced in each others' spirits and tinctures, which is the cause of this invisible sympathy.

And they that are in this near union feel a mutual indwelling in the pure tincture and life of each other. And so, the further we come out of the animal nature, the more universal we are, and nearer both to heaven, and to one another in the internal; and the further instrumentally to convey the pure streams of the heavenly life to each other, which no external distance can hinder. For the divine tincture (being such a spiritual virtue as Christ imprinted into the heart of the disciples with whom he talked after his resurrection, making their hearts to burn within them) is able to pierce through all distance, and reach those that are far absent; because it is not corporeal, nor subject to the laws of place or time.

I know of no other account quite like this, offering insights into the spiritual life of an alchemical community.

A DIFFERENT WAY OF BEING

What we are discussing here is an entirely different way of being in the world than is represented in materialistic, technological, and exploitive global society. It is a fundamentally different model, consciously created in relation to a specific place and people, with a specific religious tradition and specific locally applied folkways. It is a way of being centered on human, natural, and spiritual flourishing and on salvation, liberation, and illumination, or enlightenment.

It became commonplace for people to reflexively critique and reject cultures and traditions, especially in the academic world, so that the only acceptable model was materialistic, physicalistic, consumeristic, and individualistic. Such a model you can recognize because its premises are aligned with communism and corporationism and opposed, explicitly or implicitly, to cultures, religions, and traditions, which are often termed "backward" or "religionist" or any other pejorative someone can cook up. Instead of conserving our understanding of culture, academia became home to packs of cultural attack dogs—not preservers but destroyers. However, we need not heed these kinds of people.

We know from our collective and individual human inheritances and history that a different way of being in the world is possible. And alchemy provides many guideposts on our individual and shared journey. Alchemical works like the *Emerald Tablet* or the visions of Zosimos or the treatises of Dionysius Freher or Thomas Vaughan light our way. The mystical tradition in Christianity is long and deep. Meditation traditions such as Mahamudra and Dzogchen in Vajrayana Buddhism provide us with clear direction.*

As we've discussed throughout this book, following the stages of the alchemical path can be not only an individual undertaking but also a shared path to intentionally create couples, families, and communities that understand themselves as vessels conveying a balanced, harmonious way of life into the future, restoring the balance between the human, the natural, and the spiritual realms. This is possible.

In an age of decline, could a new Grail culture be established? If so, it would not look backward but forward. It would be animated by a shared mythos, a shared sense of its overarching meaning and purpose. It would understand itself and its people to be on a quest for their realization, which is beyond any individual, beyond a particular family or tribe, for it includes also the natural and spiritual dimensions.

---

*Mahamudra and Dzogchen are related meditation practice traditions in Tibetan Buddhism. Mahamudra texts such as *Moonbeams of Mahamudra* by Takpo Tashi Namgyal clearly detail the stages of progressive illumination and awakening, drawing on many earlier classical Buddhist masters in this tradition.

Of course, we know that unique communities could be derailed or fail. After all, Plato tells us that even great Atlantis fell. We have been so conditioned by materialism, dualism, and all manner of critiques and so deeply inculcated by pessimism from childhood on that undoubtedly we can all think of what could go wrong, of cult leaders and conflicts and reasons for dissolution before such a project has even begun.

Still, there have been and are optimistic visions. Already in the seventeenth century, the movement of the Rosy Cross, or the Rosicrucian Order,* had emerged into public view, and its adherents' vision included what could be termed invisible communities. The alchemist Thomas Vaughan wrote about the Order, comparing it to Asian communities, and remarking on the "dwelling of R. C. [the Rosy Cross; the Rosicrucians; Christian Rosenkreutz] which his followers call *Locus Sancti Spiritus*, or place of the Holy Spirit." Vaughan goes on to observe that the Order's realm was hidden to all except those who can see in the light of the spirit: "The fraternity of R. C. can move in this white mist: 'whosoever would communicate with us must be able to see in this light, or us he will never see—unless by our own will.'" Vaughan adds that there is an elite in India that also live in a hidden Elysium, both "on the earth and not on the earth."

Vaughan also provides a quoted description of a Rosicrucian realm:

> I beheld on a day the Olympian towers shining by a certain stream and famous city, which we have consecrated by the name of the Holy Spirit. I speak of Helicon, or double-peaked Parnassus, wherein the steed Pegasus opened a fountain of perennial water, flowing to this very day. Therein Diana bathes; therewith are associated Venus as a

---

*The Rosicrucian Order was announced in a series of three enigmatic texts during the early seventeenth century, generating considerable interest in European intellectual circles. Whether a Rosicrucian Order actually existed, its nature and its successors remain publicly murky to the present day. What is clear, though, is that there was a Rosicrucian vision for a spiritually inspired future and that the alchemist Thomas Vaughan shared in and participated in this vision. See for instance A. E. Waite's *The Works of Thomas Vaughan, Mystic and Alchemist*, which includes Vaughan's discussion of Rosicrucianism.

waiting-maid, and Saturn as a patient client. These are words that will say too much to those who understand, but to the inexpert little or nothing.

Of course, we can dismiss such accounts and the Rosicrucian movement as fictional. But is the vision that informs it really so easily dismissed? Certainly by materialistic cynics—yet the vision still calls to some, hinting of a different, healthier, wiser, more balanced way of being.

We know, intuitively, that new kinds of community are possible. In fact, many people already recognize that a new model, a new way of being in the world, is essential now. That's why sustainable communities are emerging in many places, quietly, all around the globe. Many have felt called to such projects, and we have seen new community initiatives going back centuries in Europe and in the European diaspora. In fact, the American frontier could be understood as such a project, on a vast scale, within which were smaller experiments such as theosophic-alchemical communities in Pennsylvania or Michigan.

And we can imagine such community experiments on new worlds. This has been hinted at in science fiction novels, films, and series, and it is after all possible. If we can envision it, it certainly could happen. But what are the organizing principles that would guide such a community? Materialism and nihilism don't lead to thriving communities. We already know that from hard experience, as modernism in the twentieth century became synonymous with the atomizing dissolution of cultures and meaning. As we have seen throughout this book, alchemy tells us that for individuals and communities to truly flourish, all three realms—human, natural, and spiritual—need to be recognized and integrated. The symbol for the integration of the three realms is the triquetra.

The triquetra shows the intersection of the vertical spiritual with the human and natural realms. This image, like alchemy itself, reflects the underlying principles inherent in the cosmos and in human beings. Alchemy gives us indications of a transformative path toward illumination. Of course, we have to walk that path for ourselves, in our own

The intersection of the spiritual, the human, and the natural symbolized in the triquetra.

circumstances and place. But the principles are inherent in who and where we are, whether on Earth or on another world.

The essence of alchemy is to restore the primordial balance between the three domains. This restoration is the final, rubedo stage. We instinctively know, on some level, that we have gone astray, that materialistic, technological society went astray long ago and that a profoundly different way of being is possible. We know that there are no technological solutions based in a materialistic, dualistic paradigm. There is no way to restore balance from inside a machine system separated from all three realms.

A primordialist movement is a return to the profound natural order. It is a return to the origin point (*ab origine*), to the restoration of harmonic balance between humanity, nature, and spirit. The result is regeneration, restoration of what was lost during the long time of going astray, away from harmonic balance. The origin point is timeless, and returning to timeless light is the transmutation and restoration. Alchemy is the process of transmutation and restoration, and primordialism describes how this process manifests culturally. Primordialism refers to the illuminated, timeless origin-point of culture as manifested in the world, integrating all three realms. Of course it is possible to go astray, to make mistakes, to become confused, or to forget. But it is also possible to remember, to reorient ourselves, to return to integration and balance.

New intentional communities are vital. There are countless paths to creating such communities, but private ownership of contiguous property is critical. In this way, the local infrastructure and local political and legal systems are much more likely to be supportive. Essentially, you're developing a unique tribal community in the sense of familial and shared religious tribes. Inevitably, there is an ethnic, which is to say ancestral bond, in communities that endure over time. The challenge is to recognize and balance both ethnic and religious commitments. Communities die when one eclipses the other.

All of this and more is conveyed in the *Emerald Tablet*, which concludes by invoking Hermes Trismegistus, who shares with us the three parts of the philosophy of the whole world. These are the three parts of spirit, nature, and human, from the union of which culture emerges. And so what he has to say concerning the operation of the Sun is completed. The Sun here is the spiritual Sun that illuminates the transmuted landscape of a new culture, as we see in the *Splendor Solis* image in the front cover of this book.

The stages of alchemy can be understood as a way to see more clearly where we are, and where we are heading. They provide us with a larger context for our own spiritual journey, for that of a couple, and for that of a community. The alchemical stages are inherent in us as human beings, and help orient us and those around us toward flourishing and spiritual awakening.

In reading or hearing these words, you are already engaged in the process of restoration. Intentionality is key. Shared intention impels and guides community. Aspiration is also key. There are small aspirations, large aspirations, and ones so vast that they can't really be comprehended. A small aspiration is particular—for this individual, that animal, this lake. A large aspiration is for all the animals, all the folk, all the spirits in the area. A vast aspiration is for all beings of every kind, visible and invisible, to be truly free and happy.

Through what is suggested in this book and in these words, may all beings of every kind, visible and invisible, awaken in light and reach liberation.

APPENDIX I

Additional Resources

At the nonprofit Hieros Institute, we have created a course complementary to this book called Gathering Light. This is a unique course on alchemy, spiritual awakening, and creating healthier, more balanced, and more profound communities and cultures. In this course, we offer some ways to explore more deeply who we are and how we are in this natural world. Among these are what we have come to call experiments. These experiments are ways of deepening our understanding of how the three domains—nature, humanity, and spirit—intersect with one another. They are ways of coming to more deeply understand primordial nature, primordial humanity, and primordial spirits. They also are ways of returning to the essence or timeless origin point of culture, which means seeing things anew, primordially. These experiments are meant for individuals but in the larger context of coexploration. We need to recover our deeper connections to archaic and primordial sources of inner understanding.

Gathering Light is closely related to another course, called The Short Way: A Christian Mystical Path, that draws on a remarkably clear and succinct guidebook by the great mystic Jacob Böhme to offer an introduction to meditative alchemical practice. This course, with accompanying recorded guidance, draws on images and text for weekly meditative practices in the alchemical tradition. As far as we know, this is the first time such resources have been made available for deepening one's work in this profound tradition.

And there also is a course called Becoming Conscious that goes much more extensively into experimental exploration of who we are and of the nature of nature, drawing on our shared human inheritance of great classical literature, music, art, and theater. This course is about deepening our understanding of how the liberal arts are really about liberation, meaning the awakening of consciousness that goes beyond our own selfhood, beyond our own particular time and society, into wider and deeper understanding.

Videos, additional courses, and other resources can be found on the Hieros Institute website. Such resources have been rare or invisible in the past, but as new coexplorers and new communities continue to develop, more may appear, in different venues and forms. We see the Hieros Institute as a venue and forum for encouraging and supporting these vital initiatives.

APPENDIX 2

An Alchemical Community

There have been small communities dedicated to spiritual awakening over recent centuries, some larger, some smaller, many not well known. There were communities dedicated to a shared spiritual life in England, in Germany, and in the United States from the seventeenth century onward, but most are little known even today. Others developed as a result of Buddhism taking root in the Americas. Such communities spring up when there is a shared aspiration for spiritual practice and awakening, sometimes in the mountains or in places off the beaten track. What is it like to visit the kind of alchemical community discussed in this book? Here is the beginning of one account.

We had heard tell that they were different, but no one we knew had actually been there. You know how it is. People keep to themselves these days, often out of fear. I remember meeting a young man who had never travelled the forty or fifty miles from his town across the border. Most people tend to stay put, especially now, with all the controls they put in place. It isn't easy to find things out, or even to talk freely. But you know all that, of course.

Then by chance I met one of them, a young blonde woman, when I was out hiking in the wild backcountry. I came across her unexpectedly, and we got to talking. Mayda, she said her name was. She told me about her people, and I was keen to meet them. She said

I could come to visit the following Saturday, maybe in midmorning, and told me how to get there. You can bet I did.

That Saturday, on a new Moon, with Venus still barely visible, I set out. To get there, I took to the road going north, when the dew was still glistening on the grass alongside it. I walked for some miles, through rural countryside, past woods and rolling fields, until I reached the crossroad she had mentioned. It was marked, just as she had said, by a stone column with a square base, at the top an offset cylindrical oval shape. At the base were some blue flowers. I took the crossroad heading west, toward the western end of high hills below which a river ran through a valley.

The land here was forested, and this was the area where I had met Mayda. I hadn't realized that her people owned nearly all the forested land through which I was passing; I had gotten the wrong impression somehow it was public land. So much wild land like this was itself unusual. The trees were wide and tall, mature hardwoods, some of great age. Ahead of me, off to the side, I saw movement: a red fox, hunting alongside the road. With unfathomable eyes, he looked sharply at me, an unexpected interloper here. Then he vanished into the woods. I felt as though he was a kind of sentinel, perhaps also a companion. I heard the scree of what I think was an eagle, wheeling somewhere overhead.

I came to the road into the forest she had described, wide and brown, on each side of it stone columns like the one I had seen earlier, though these were larger and more ornate. The elder trees were high above this road, making it more dim, as if a little night still clung to it. Unlike most roads I knew, this one was serpentine, and you could never quite predict what lay ahead on each turn, sometimes a creek, sometimes a high point or a hollow. I thought I saw a stag between the trees ahead of me, with a great rack of antlers, but when I looked again, it was gone. And then, past the trees, I could see the homes in the distance. I knew instantly that here were Mayda's people.

Beyond the woods there were fields, with greyed split rail fencing, and animals grazing. Cattle here, some horses over there. There were houses hither and yon, of designs I'd not seen before, each one distinctive. Each had barns and outbuildings, so each was clearly a farmstead, and most had small orchards and several gardens. Ahead was a larger building, circular, windows all around, with a high cupola in the center, and there were children playing in a grassy area near it. As I passed, I thought I could see library stacks in the center, with many books.

Ahead was a village, the homes still surrounded by green, but closer together, and there were some shops and other buildings. There was a grocer and various other stores that seemed well-stocked, and I wondered how. Did they trade, or did these folk make most of their own goods? Then there was a larger building on Main Street, with a sign reading "Smithy," and it was evident they worked with metals. Various tools and implements were visible outside and inside, some quite large. Then there was another larger building, with a sign reading "The Forge," and through the doorway I was surprised to see what looked like machinery and computers, certainly technology. The arcadian look of the area had made me think they had eschewed technology, but evidently not entirely.

Mayda's family home was on the far side of town, down a curving lane. I knew which one because she'd said it would have a golden and blue flag with a crest to mark it. It was a white house with pillars, and had a more classical look than many of the others. In the yard, several little girls were playing, watched over by a dark-haired teen girl who was reading a book with her back to a tree. She looked up.

"I'm here to see Mayda," I said.

"She's expecting you," she said. "I'll let her know you're here."

"Thank you."

She left the book under the tree and bustled into the house through a door around the side. The little girls were playing with intricate little dolls and a dollhouse, so engrossed that they took no notice of me. It struck me that their play was a miniature version of this whole area, which seemed to exist in a bubble, taking no notice of the outside world, while the outside world took no notice of it. I half expected to glimpse an actual bubble half-visible in the air.

"Greetings."

It was Mayda, greeting me with a bright smile, coming down the main steps of the house from under the pillars.

"Not too long a walk to get here, was it?"

"No, and now I'm surprised I've never been here before. It's not far, and yet it's like another world," I said.

"So it is. Shall I show you around?"

"Please do. I'm most curious."

"We could start with the library and school. Would you like something to drink before we go?"

"I would, if you'll have some too."

"Of course. Tea?"

She disappeared into the house, and returned, after a while, carrying a tray with two steaming teacups and two pastries that resembled golden-brown croissants. She set the tray on the lawn under a large oak tree, and we sat together with our backs to the tree. The pastries were delicious, light and airy, but with a tart-sweet filling.

"The tea is our own, from mint and other herbs."

The tea's scent and taste was quite distinctively pungent, and I complimented it, and the remarkable pastries.

"My grandmother's recipe," she said.

When we had finished, and she'd returned the tray and teacups, we walked together back up the drive and toward the village.

"How did this place come to be here?" I asked, as we walked toward Main Street and its paired lines of buildings, rather like in the American Old West, I realized.

"It came about because several families purchased land here at the same time, with the intention of creating this. We kept purchasing land as we were able, jointly or individually, and we brought in others of like mind as time went on."

"What connects people here? Was it strictly friendships?" I inquired. Mayda looked at me and paused before replying.

"There's much more to it, but it's not easy to explain to an outsider. Be patient, and perhaps you'll begin to see."

As we walked along Main Street toward the library, I noticed that everyone visible seemed to know her, and they greeted one another with an unusual gesture, making a fist and holding it at the heart. She did the same.

We paused at the smithy's, as a very burly man with a florid face and thick arms, wearing a leather smock, greeted her warmly.

"Greetings, Mayda," he said as they each brought their fist to the heart.

"Greetings, Weyland." She smiled at him. "Good to see you. How is the project coming?"

"The metal is consecrated, and we're on our way. Sometime early next week, I think."

"Weyland is making something special for my father. It's a particular kind of knife, with a rainbow in the blade. The handle is from a stag antler. Not an ordinary stag; this one goes between the worlds."

"Between the worlds?"

"Yes, haven't you heard of that? Some call it a deer cult, and it's very ancient. We understand that deer can move between worlds in a very special way, disappearing in one and reappearing in another. We call them the spirit animal. It's said a deer guided our ancestors here," she continued.

Weyland looked at me penetratingly, sizing up my response to this, but said nothing.

"His work is very beautiful, as you will see," Mayda said. "My father said there is a special purpose for this dagger. But he hasn't told us what it is."

"How is he doing?" asked Weyland.

"He's still ailing," she replied. "About the same."

"I see," said Weyland. "When you return, perhaps I will be able to show you something."

We walked on to the library building, and entered through a large wooden door, above it and around it a stone arch. The building, now that we were here, appeared to have been made largely out of local wood and stone, and although it looked to have been constructed relatively recently, it had an ancient quality to it, as though it had been here for a thousand years already. Inside, there was a high wooden ceiling lit by a ring of windows above, and then another ring below. The books were on wooden shelving, and while some books were modern, others appeared to be leather bound and ancient.

"Our library is very unusual, I think. My great-granduncle was a scholar with many interests. One of them was alchemy, so he set about collecting many resources for its study. We have also a laboratory. The school adjoins the library. Students are encouraged to pursue their passionate interests and explore, and they also learn what we call core knowledge."

"Can I have a look?" I asked.

"Of course," said Madya.

The books were organized in an unfamiliar way, but clearly were grouped by area. There was one section on Christian mysticism, with titles including Dionysius the Areopagite, Meister Eckhart, and Jacob Böhme, with volumes in the original German as well as an array of English translations, Dionysius Freher, and other classics. There was a section of Tibetan Buddhist works, including a multivolume series called The Treasury of Knowledge by Jamgon Kongtrul, and many other titles.

"It seems to be organized by areas of knowledge," I said.

"Just so. You're in the religion section, which is the most extensive, but there are sections on all manner of subjects. Let's go upstairs, as there's something you should see."

She guided me to a spiral staircase that took us up to a second floor, where we were surrounded by windows so we could see the valley around us, in the distance the river's shining serpentine course, fields and farms, and the village all spread out around us.

"This area is for contemplation," Madya said. "Even as children, we're encouraged to come here, read, and contemplate. We learn to meditate at a young age. It's integrated into our school life."

"I'm not totally sure what you're talking about. We never learned anything like that where I'm from."

"I know we're different. But over time, you begin to understand more clearly. That's how it is with us, too. It's just that we start earlier, and we have a shared perspective on life."

"What does that mean, exactly?" We sat in bentwood rocking chairs near the windows. They were surprisingly comfortable. They were clearly handmade out of limbs that had been carefully shaped, some with bark, others with the slats more polished and lighter.

"It's hard to explain, more something you slowly begin to comprehend over time. It's a vast vision we share. Some of us have gone deeper than others. But we're all on a path of illumination."

"Are you Christian?"

"Yes, but it's a Christianity of the path of light. We also can be said to be Pagan and Buddhist."

"So it's a synthesis?"

"Not exactly. More like we share an alchemical understanding, and these traditions help us understand and realize that more deeply. And to be more connected to nature and to the invisible ones so nearby but largely unseen. There's someone you could meet if you come back who can explain much better than I can. We call him Brother Thomas. He lives on the other side of the river, up on the mountain in a cabin near a little chapel there."

"He's a recluse?"

"You could call him that. Or a hermit. Although he does often have visitors, probably more than he likes."

We descended the spiral staircase and Mayda took me past the school and out a side door into the bright sunshine.

"I've never even heard of such a community as this," I said.

"We are small and happy. We live simple lives. One key is that collectively, we own this whole area. We can largely live as we please. In school, we learned a bit about how people went astray in the past, pursuing all manner of distractions and destruction of nature. Our ancestors were determined not to repeat those disastrous errors."

"How did you achieve this?" I asked.

"We aren't part of the system, and for the most part, from their perspective, we don't exist."

"But how is that possible?" I asked, startled.

"For one thing," she replied, "we have runners. They have digital currency accounts and exist in the outside system for us. For another, we are relatively self-sufficient. We raise animals, grow food, and have many small shops and manufactories. And we trade with others in our confederacy. We support one another."

During that first visit, Mayda took me to several shops and what she called "manufactories," and I got the clear sense that despite the arcadian look of the place, there was far more here than one could discover in a multitude of visits, even perhaps years of living there.

I felt intuitively that these quiet, industrious, laconic people had mysteries within mysteries in their small community. And I felt that they were free in ways that I had never seen before, or even knew was possible. Having lived my whole life in a very different kind of society, one where virtually everything was proscribed and controlled, I was profoundly drawn to this place and these people, who had managed to be somehow invisible for all these years. How had they accomplished this?

There was so much that I wanted to learn and understand. Unexpectedly, a wholly new future vista, a new world, had opened before me. Alchemy? Light? Mysticism? Crafts? Old gods and spirits? Who were these people? Even before I took my leave, I couldn't wait to come back to this idyllic place and see Mayda again.

APPENDIX 3

Dialogues and Illumination

The following dialogue was taken from William Law's edition of Jacob Böhme's *Dialogues on the Supersensual Life*, a remarkable, lucid treatise on spiritual illumination. Details on this edition of the book can be found in the *Further Readings* section. Note that I have modernized the language slightly here to make it more accessible.

DISCIPLE: I know that I cannot do it of myself. But I would like to learn how I must receive this divine light and grace into me. What is then required of me in order to admit this breaker of the partition and to promote the attainment of the ends of such admission?

MASTER: There is nothing more required of you at first than not to resist this grace manifested in you, and nothing in the whole process of your work but to be obedient and passive to the light of God shining through the darkness of your creaturely being, which comprehends it not, as reaching no higher than the light of nature.

DISCIPLE: But is it not for me to attain, if I can, both the light of God, and the light of the outward nature too: and to make use of them both for ordering my life wisely and prudently?

MASTER: It is right to do so. And it is indeed a treasure above all earthly treasures, to be possessed of the light of God and nature, operating in their spheres; and to have both the eye of time and eternity at once open together, and yet not to interfere with each other.

DISCIPLE: This is a great satisfaction to me to hear; having been very uneasy about it for some time. But how this can be without interfering with each other, there is the difficulty: wherefore fain would I know, if it were lawful, the boundaries of the one and the other; and how both the divine and the natural light may in their several spheres respectively act and operate, for the manifestation of the mysteries of God and nature, and for the conduct of my outward and inward life?

MASTER: That each of these may be preserved distinct in their several spheres, without confounding things heavenly and things earthly, or breaking the golden chain of wisdom, it will be necessary, my child, in the first place to wait for and attend the supernatural and divine light, as that superior light appointed to govern the day, rising in the true east, which is the center of paradise; and in great might breaking forth as out of the darkness within you, through a pillar of fire and thunder clouds, and thereby also reflecting upon the inferior light of nature a sort of image of itself, whereby only it can be kept in its due subordination, that which is below being made subservient to that which is above; and that which is without to that which is within. Thus there will be no danger of interfering; but all will go right, and everything abide in its proper sphere.

DISCIPLE: Therefore, unless reason or the light of nature be sanctified in my soul, and illuminated by this superior light, as from the central east of the holy lightworld, by the eternal and intellectual sun; I perceive there will be always some confusion, and I shall never be able to manage aright either what concerns time or eternity: but I must always be at a loss, or break the links of wisdom's chain.

MASTER: It is even so as you have said. All is confusion, if you have no more but the dim light of nature, or unsanctified and unregenerate reason to guide you by; and if only the eye of time be opened in you, which cannot pierce beyond its own limit. Wherefore seek the fountain of light, waiting in the deep ground of your soul for the rising there of the sun of righteousness, whereby the light of nature in you, with the properties thereof, will be made to shine seven times brighter than ordinary. For it shall receive the stamp, image, and impression of the supersensual and supernatural; so that the sensual and rational life will hence be brought into the most perfect order and harmony.

DISCIPLE: But how am I to wait for the rising of this glorious sun, and how am I to seek in the center, this fountain of light, which may enlighten me throughout, and bring all my properties into perfect harmony? I am in nature as I said before; and which way shall I pass through nature, and the light thereof, so that I may come into that supernatural and supersensual ground, whence this true light, which is the light of minds, does arise; and this, without the destruction of my nature, or quenching the light of it, which is my reason?

MASTER: Cease but from your own activity, steadfastly fixing your eye upon one point, and with a strong purpose relying upon the promised grace of God in Christ, to bring you out of your darkness into his marvelous light. For this end gather in all your thoughts, and by faith press into the center, laying hold upon the word of God, which is infallible, and which has called you. Be you then obedient to this call; and be silent before the lord, sitting alone with him in your inmost and most hidden cell, your mind being centrally united in itself, and attending his will in the patience of hope. So shall your light break forth as the morning; and after the redness thereof is passed, the sun himself, which you wait for, shall arise unto you, and under his most healing wings you shall greatly rejoice; ascending and descending in his bright and healing beams. Behold this is the true supersensual ground of life.

DISCIPLE: But how shall I comprehend it?

MASTER: If you go about to comprehend it, then it will fly away from you; but if you surrender yourself wholly up to it, then it will abide with you, and become the life of your life, and be natural to you.

The following selection was taken from a seventeenth-century work by Thomas Bromley titled *The Way to the Sabbath of Rest* that offers some insight into the inner life of a spiritual community to which he belonged. Of particular note is his mention of how spiritual community can transcend the usual boundaries of time and space.

> I here give directions to those who having attained constant habitual communion with God, press after perfection.
>
> And certainly there is no better way than from the annihilation of all thoughts, and the retiring from the fantasy into the silent mind, which more fits the soul for divine irradiation and spiritual embraces; for the more quiet we are, the less resistance we make against a supernatural impression, and the easier we perceive the beginning of divine attraction, and so yield ourselves to it. And truly, when the soul hath attained the power to throw itself into the silent super-imaginary state (which must be attained by the habitual constant practice of it) it will then come to internal openings, and intellectual sights of the invisible world, and many times receive quickening glances from eternity, with those strong infusions of love that bring the soul many times near to a rapture. And truly, the enjoyment we have in this state fully recompenses all that self-denial we pass through to the attainment of it.
>
> Here then the false prophet (which is irregular imagination) comes to be conquered, being commanded by the inward mind that now oft draws up the soul into the paradisical world, from the motion of fantasy and imagination.
>
> Imagination being now overcome, and the animal man mortified, the soul cannot but clearly discover its growth into the image of God, and the resurrection of the angelical man, which now evidently perceives itself springing up in a new principle, above the spirit of the world [*spiritus mundi*], and its mixed laws. And here we come to own and receive new relations contracted in our progress in the new birth, and our [movement] from the spirit of the world toward eternity.

But we shall here find a nearer union and communion among those who have been by one particular instrument begotten into the life of Christ, having a peculiar vein of spiritual enjoyment running through them; which others, who received not that particular tincture, do not partake of. And had we lived in the apostle's times, we should have seen this among the primitive Christians . . . [for] amongst those who are thus peculiarly united, we . . . see some more closely knit in spiritual agreement than others, and essenced into one another's spirits. . . .

For grace and the work of regeneration do not destroy our natural signatures, only rectify them by that heavenly principle, which [translates] all our spirits into the highest perfection they are capable of, by their primary model and frame. Hence it appears that they are more truly brethren (even according to natural nature) who thus agree, and correspond in their essences, than they who are ordinarily called so, who are many times very contrary signatured. And the reason of this assertion is that, when our natures come to their perfect rectitude and restoration by union with God; this secret propensity and harmonious closing with those that are like essenced, remains; whereas from mere natural relation there nothing continues; though in those who are related, there may be this agreement too.

Mere relation is not the cause of it, but [rather] that secret law of influence, which God has established to signature some one way, some another; some in much agreement and proportion; others more differing, though all representing something of that variety, which is wrapt up in the unity of the eternal nature. I could not but give a hint of this, because it may open some things concerning relations, which may lie dark to those who know not the deepest ground and root of them.

But I shall proceed to the further opening of those enjoyments, which flow from union with new relations, which come now to be very dear, because the ground of the relation is so pure and good, being not of man, but of God. Here we shall experience the happy effects of our pure union, which produces that divine love that none can know, but those that enjoy it. But this will be strongest, where there is most harmony and agreement in spirits and natures; because the eternal tincture works upon and through everything according to its nature and capacity. Hence we come to enjoy more from some, than others; and some from us receive more than others. But that brotherly love and friendship, which now comes to be renewed in spirit, far transcends any enjoyments merely natural. And whatsoever we parted with, in dying to all earthly affection and its objects, we regain in the resurrection of our spirits, in this pure love, which is not affection, but something above it; not consisting in sudden outflowings and eruptions, but in a constant sweet inclination and secret propensity of the spirit, to those which are one with it, in the pure life. And this good-willingness is so great that from it the soul could give its life (or if there were anything dearer than life) for its brother; and choose sufferings, to free others from them. In this state there will be a sympathizing in joy and sorrow; and where the union is eminently great, there may be some knowledge of each others' conditions at a distance, which comes from their being essenced in each others' spirits and tinctures, which is the cause of this invisible sympathy.

And they that are in this near union feel a mutual indwelling in the pure tincture and life of each other. And so, the further we come out of the animal nature, the more universal we are, and nearer both to heaven, and to one another in the internal; and the further instrumentally to convey the pure streams of the heavenly life to each other, which no external distance can hinder. For the divine tincture (being such a spiritual virtue as Christ imprinted into the heart of the disciples with whom he talked after his resurrection, making their hearts to burn within them) is able to pierce through all distance, and reach those that are far absent; because it is not corporeal, nor subject to the laws of place or time.

Now this is known to some by experience, who in absence enjoy such influences of spirit and secret [inspirations] of spiritual virtue from one another, that they cannot but value this spiritual communion above all enjoyments in the world; which compared to it, seem but like the basest metal to the purest gold. . . .

And though some (who think they have passed far in the new birth) have experienced this; and may therefore look upon it as a thing not much to be regarded; yet let all such know that the reason may be, in that they never yet passed clear out of the spirit of the world, nor overcame their animal nature by a complete renunciation; and so were not capable to receive any extraordinary enjoyment of visions, revelations, in-speaking, prophecies, unions of spirits; and being not come into this inward wilderness, where the soul is fitted for such things, and where these spiritual temptations arise to try it. . . .

But they that have come so far in the work of the new birth as to be acquainted with, and to live with these things, must of necessity die to them, and come to be nothing in them, given up all to God. . . .

By this time the soul experiences the happy state of being freed from the principle of selfness in returning to God from the spirit of the world, and sees the real progress it has made from the outward through the inward dark world into the internal paradise, where Adam lived before his Fall, and where Christ conversed betwixt the time of his resurrection and ascension. In this spiritual region, the curse is not manifest, there being a perpetual spring. Here are the ideas of all visible bodies, in much beauty and appealing luster. Here are those bright clouds, which overshadowed Christ on the mount, and when he was received up into heaven; in which he will descend, when he comes again to judge the earth.

Now the soul, having attained to the state of this angelical garden, knows what it is to turn and become as a child and to attain a secret and quiet life of innocence and pure love, free from those passions and evil affections it had formerly groaned under. And here it experiences what it is to be born of water and the spirit, as a necessary qualification to do the will of God. And sees its conception in the womb of wisdom, (which is our new mother) who here distills the milk of the eternal word, (from the eternal world) to feed and nourish the soul. Whither it now travels, fixing its sight upon that pure river of water of life, clear as crystal, proceeding out of the throne of God, and of the Lamb. But now likewise the soul lives the life of spiritual vegetation, and grows like a willow by the water-courses, or a lily in the garden of the Lord, being continually refreshed with the dews of the eternal heavens and quickened by the beams of the sun of righteousness, and cherished with the enlivening gates of the holy spirit. All that are in this state, are like the harmless flowers in a fruitful garden springing from the same ground, yet differing in color, virtue, smell, and growth, according to their several natures and times of planting; yet all serving to express the power, love, and wisdom of their creator, without any strife or contention for eminent place or esteem, being all satisfied with what God affords them, and their different capacities fit them.

Further Readings

Böhme, Jacob. *Dialogues on the Supersensual Life*. William Law, ed., online at Project Gutenberg or in the course The Short Way online at Hieros Institute.

———. *The Signature of All Things*. London: James Clarke, 1912/1969.

Bromley, Thomas. *The Way to the Sabbath of Rest*. London: 1678. Reprinted Germantown: Christopher Sower, 1759.

Dowman, Keith, trs., *Masters of Mahamudra: Songs and Histories of the Eighty-four Buddhist Siddhas*. Albany: SUNY Press, 1986.

Faas, Robert J. *The Divine Couple: A Christian Book of Mystery on Eros-Love*. Minneapolis: Grailstone, 2001.

Faas, Robert J. and Arthur Versluis. *Conversations in Apocalyptic Times*. Minneapolis: Grailstone, 2021.

Musès, Charles. *Illumination on Jacob Boehme: The Work of Dionysius Andreas Freher*. New York: Kings Crown, 1951.

Namgyal, Takpo Tashi. *Moonbeams of Mahamudra*. Ithaca, NY: Snow Lion, 2019.

Plotinus. *Enneads*. A. H. Armstrong, trs. Cambridge, MA: Harvard University Press, 1966.

———. *The Enneads*. Stephen MacKenna, trs. Internet Archive.

Scot, Patrick. *The Tillage of Light, or, A True Discoverie of the Philosophicall Elixir, Commonly Called the Philosophers Stone*. London: William Lee, 1623.

Stewart, R. J. *Earth Light: The Ancient Path to Transformation*. R. J. Stewart Books, 2024.

Vaughan, Thomas. *The Works of Thomas Vaughan*. Edited by Alan Rudrum. New York: Oxford University Press, 1984 (earlier editions available online).

Versluis, Arthur. *American Gnosis: Political Religion and Transcendence*. New York: Oxford University Press, 2023.

———. *Entering the Mysteries: The Secret Traditions of Indigenous Europe*. Minneapolis: New Cultures Press, 2016.

———. *Platonic Mysticism: Contemplative Science, Philosophy, Literature, and Art*. Albany: SUNY Press, 2017.

———. *The Mystical State: Politics, Gnosis, and Emergent Cultures*. Minneapolis: New Cultures Press, 2011.

———. *The Secret History of Western Sexual Mysticism*. Rochester, VT: Inner Traditions, 2008.

Index

Agathodaemon, 22–23
albedo (white), 36
alchemy, 4–5, 20–29, 60, 61, 64, 65–70, 81–83, 88–90, 101–2, 119–26
alternative communities (Hermetic, Platonic, Brotherhood of New Life, Distributist) 119
Amish, 118
Apuleius, *The Golden Ass*, 70
archaic cultures, 54–55
arithmosophy, 86–87
astral shell, 30–38
astrology, 66, 117
Atlantis, 63, 123
Aurora Consurgens, 7, 68

Bhutan, 13, 63, 85, 99–100, 106, 108
   Tiger's Nest, 85
Böhme, Jacob, 6, 14, 32, 63, 80, 90, 106, 137–44
   Dialogues on the Supersensual Life, 91–92, 137–44
   Signature of All Things, 14
Bön, 99–100
Brittany, 108

Bromley, Thomas, 120–21
   The Way to the Sabbath of Rest, 120–21, 140–44
Buddhism, 19, 65, 97, 99–100, 129
   Nyingma Buddhism, 78, 116
   Vajrayana Buddhism, 70, 78, 79, 106

candeo (white), 36
carapace of conditioning, 34–38
chakras, 90
Chaldean Oracles, 79
Chinese communism, 15
Christ, 43, 45, 68, 70, 85, 87, 89
Christian Mysteries, 43, 70, 80
Christian mysticism, 6, 33, 70
Christianity, 54, 68, 70, 80, 85, 106
citrinitas (yellow), 76
communism, 15
culture, 95–98, 105–6

dark age, 44–45
Dionysius the Areopagite, 106
dreams, 1
Drukpa Kunley, 100
Dzogchen, 122

Index

Eckhart, Meister, 106
ecovillages, 2
egregore, 40–41
Emerald Tablet, 1, 5, 7, 33, 35, 38, 46, 48, 52, 57, 59, 68, 81, 87, 103, 108, 110, 111–12, 122, 126
enlightenment, 8, 97
Erigena, John Scotus, 106

fairy tales, 113
Flue, Nicholas von, 100
Freher, Dionysius Andreas, 65, 68, 80, 122
future archaic, 96

Gathering Light (course), 127
GNH (Gross National Happiness), 13
gnosis, 31
Golden Age, 18–19
grailstone, 59, 62
Grail tradition, 9–10, 28, 59, 64, 112, 122
Greek Orthodoxy, 85
Guru Rinpoche (Padmasambhava), 45, 70, 85–86, 109–10

Hermes Trismegistus (Thrice-Great Hermes), 5, 45, 57, 68, 70, 111–12, 126
Hermetic tradition, 6, 44, 50, 81
hidden lands (beyul), 108–10
Hieros Institute, 127–28
Hinduism, 19
house of light, 49

initiation, 4–5
Ireland, 114
Iron Age, 18, 86

Jigme Singye Wangchuck, 13

Kali Yuga, 18, 86

Law, William, 63, 91, 137–44
light communities, 118–21
light of nature (lumen naturae), 48–56
lightworking, 3

MacKenna, Stephen, 27
Magna Mater (Great Mother), 77
Mahamudra, 100, 122
mahasiddhas, 27
materialism, 16, 17–19, 31
meteoric iron, 6
millenarianism, 37
mortification, 24–25
multidimensionality, 3
Mysteries, 42–43, 48, 76–83
   Eleusinian, 77
   Orphic, 77, 78
   Samothracian, 76, 77, 107

Nagarjuna the alchemist, 27–29, 73
New Age, 3, 37
Ngakpa, 78
nigredo (black), 14, 15, 16, 24, 36
nihilism, 17–18

One, 26–27, 78, 86
Orphism, 97

Paganism, 105–6, 116
Paracelsus, 49
Parzival, 9, 28
path of light, 1
philosopher's stone, 59, 62, 87
planets, 66–68, 69, 70
Plato, 27, 117, 123
Platonism, 50, 81
Plotinus, 26–27, 69, 91, 117
   Enneads, 27, 91
Poimandres, 44–45
Poimandres, 23, 44–45
Primordialism, 95–98, 102

quantum physics, 3

relationship (alchemical), 71–72
Rosarium Philosophorum, 7, 68, 71–72, 88–90
Rosicrucianism, 123
rubedo (red), 97

Saraha, 28
"Seventh Letter," 27
Shambhala, 108
Short Way, The (course), 127
spirit of this world, 33
spiritual families, 104–5
Splendor Solis, 7, 68, 72, 73, 92, 126

standing stones, 61, 106
steps of light, 24
Stewart, R. J., 52, 56
Switzerland, 100

technology, 41
Taoism, 116
Tibetan Buddhism, 27, 70, 73, 117
Tibetan Book of the Dead, 79
triquetra, 125

Vaughan, Thomas, 48–51, 57, 122, 123–124
   Aula Lucis, 49
Versluis, Arthur
   Entering the Mysteries, 42, 77, 107
   The Mystical State, 100
   Platonic Mysticism,
   Religion of Light, 79
   The Secret Island, 107

Western Europe, 32

Yeats, William Butler, 109

Zosimos, 21–25, 44, 57, 86, 122
   Visions, 21

About the Author

Arthur Versluis is the author of many books on subjects ranging from mysticism and magic to religion, literature, and politics. His other titles published by Inner Traditions include *Sacred Earth* and *The Secret History of Western Sexual Mysticism*. Versluis is president of the Hieros Institute, a nonprofit organization devoted to understanding and realizing the sacred in contemporary life that hosts online courses, workshops, and articles, as well as conversations with leading authors deeply engaged in spirituality and cultural renewal. He lives in rural Michigan.

For more information, visit the Hieros Institute website at **hieros.institute** or the author's website, **arthurversluis.com**.

BOOKS OF RELATED INTEREST

The Hermetic Tradition
Symbols and Teachings of the Royal Art
by Julius Evola

Drawing from sources throughout the Western esoteric tradition, Evola shows that alchemy is a universal science of transformation.

The Way of Hermes
New Translations of The Corpus Hermeticum and
The Definitions of Hermes Trismegistus to Asclepius
Translated by Clement Salaman, Dorine van Oyen, William D. Wharton, and Jean-Pierre Mahé

The Way of Hermes includes the first English translation of the recently rediscovered manuscript of *The Definitions of Hermes Trismegistus to Asclepius*. This new translation of *The Corpus Hermeticum* is of enormous value to the contemporary student of Gnostic studies.

Alchemical Hermeticism
The Secret Teachings of Marco Daffi on Initiation
by David Pantano
Foreword by Valerio Tomassini, N.D.

In this comprehensive look at the man born Baron Ricciardo Ricciardelli yet better known by his spiritual name Marco Daffi, historian and researcher David Pantano presents Daffi's writings on his unique and unusual experiences from five decades of alchemical and hermetic practice, available for the first time in English.

Scan the QR code and save 25% at InnerTraditions.com. Browse over 2,000 titles on spirituality, the occult, ancient mysteries, new science, holistic health, and natural medicine.

— SINCE 1975 • ROCHESTER, VERMONT —

InnerTraditions.com • (800) 246-8648